The World's Greatest Motor Competitions

The Monte Carlo Rally

The World's Greatest Motor Competitions

The Monte Carlo Rally

Graham Robson

B. T. Batsford Ltd, London

Photographs supplied by Colin Taylor Productions

FIRST PUBLISHED 1989
© *Miura Publications Ltd.*

ISBN 0 7134 5924 7

PRODUCED BY MIURA PUBLICATIONS LTD.
TYPESET BY PHOTOSETTING, YEOVIL
PRINTED IN ENGLAND BY WINCANTON LITHO, WINCANTON, SOMERSET
FOR THE PUBLISHERS
B. T. BATSFORD LTD
4 FITZHARDINGE STREET, LONDON, W1H 0AH

Contents

Introduction

At the top of the Col du Turini it is party time. No matter that it is 2 a.m., that this is January in the French Alps, and that the temperature is well below freezing – for a modern rallying enthusiast there is no other place to be. It might have taken hours to drive to the 5,000 ft. summit of the Col, it might have taken ages to find a parking spot, and there will certainly be thousands of other spectators confined behind the advertising barriers – but every year *this* is where Monte Carlo rally history is made.

The wait has been tedious – and cold – but at last the stage is set, and the last ice-notes crew has been waved aside. TV crews set up their cameras, microphones are checked, arc lamps are lit, and the self-important French police stride to and fro. Except for the multi-lingual chattering of French, Italian, German, British and Scandinavian spectators, all is still.

Suddenly, in the distance, a blaze of headlamps sweeps across the sky. Seconds later the first bark of a powerful rally car's engine is heard. Then, after a short but feverish delay, with the watchers' hubbub increasing all the time, a brightly liveried car bursts into view, its nose ablaze with lights, well sideways with studded-tyres scrabbling for grip. Even though there is snow and ice on the ground, the car is going far faster than expected – within seconds, perhaps with a passing swipe at a snow bank, it is over the top, through the pool of light, and racing down towards the end of the stage. In every way, this is a magnificent *coup de théâtre*.

The crowd cheers, the stop watches begin their ghostly electronic progress on hundreds of wrists, and the arguments begin. Didier, Walter, Hannu, Markku, Juha is surely going to win, lose, break down, crash, disappear . . . One minute later the next car arrives, and the cheering begins all over again.

This, then, is the excitement, the high technology, and the show-business appeal of the modern Monte Carlo rally. For the motor industry perhaps it is no longer the most important rally in the world, but it still has the most romantic reputation. Perhaps a manufacturer can be prouder of winning the Safari, and a driver can be happier to win the Lombard-RAC, but *this* is the only rally recognised by every man, in every street, in every country in Europe.

It wasn't always like that. Way back, in 1910, the Monte Carlo authorities were desperate to extend the 'season' in their tiny Principality, and to do this they promoted the idea of a glamorous winter 'rally to the sun'. It was a good idea, but one which was slow to catch on. After two very tentative attempts to build an instant tradition, the rally was abandoned, and it was a further 12 years before anyone tried again.

After 1924, however, the event established itself. By the end of the 1920s its reputation had spread to many other countries (not for nothing did the rally organisers arrange for starting points to be spread around the Continent!), and by the 1930s there were famous names in the entry lists, with the more sporting manufacturers taking an interest.

Right from the start there was a great deal of glamour and excitement attached to the Monte Carlo rally. For a competitor, the excitement came in planning the route, then successfully battling through to the Mediterranean, often in a most unsuitable car.

Even though there was no glamour involved in driving for days, often without food, and usually without sleep, there was a great deal in the arrival on the quayside in Monte Carlo, in strolling around this tiny sovereign state in winter sunshine, and in getting involved in all the post-event ceremonial. In short, for the motoring enthusiast, there was no other place to be, at that time of the year.

Once the mass media – newspapers, radio stations and (in post-Hitler war years) the TV networks – discovered the Monte Carlo rally, it

In the 1930s, there always seemed to be a lot of snow on the Monte, and the open cars had very sketchy weather protection. This was Donald Healey's 4½-litre Invicta, ready to tackle the 1933 event.

automatically became Big News. For the world's press the combination of fast cars, sport, intrigue and occasional chicanery could always be linked to the Ruritanian attractions of Monte Carlo, the opportunities for gambling, high-living and general letting-down of hair. Even in high-summer this would have been a wonderful opportunity, but in January when the rest of Europe was only interested

in burst pipes and income tax bills, it was irresistible. In any case, at that time of the year a journalist would rather be in the sunshine, on the Riviera, rather than back in a stuffy office...

Over the years, like any other long-established motoring event, the Monte Carlo rally has changed completely. What began, in the 1910s, as a gentle challenge to motorists, merely to reach the Principality, turned into the high-speed, high-technology, winter race of the 1980s. The first speed-with-regularity tests, on icy roads, came along in the 1920s, and the first sea-front driving tests followed in the 1930s.

From 1949 the old traditions increasingly jarred against the new breed of drivers, and factory teams. Drivers who had practised for weeks, had a choice of winter-treaded and studded tyres, and were backed by a service umbrella, chafed against handicapping, accurate average-speed keeping and secret checks. There was something incongruous, too, about a *Concours de Confort* competition (with whiffs of between-wars indolence) being held at the same time as factory teams were striving for rally honours and the increased sales which followed.

From the late 1950s, therefore, the organisers gradually fell into line with the rest of the rallying world. The last *Concours* was held in 1958, while secret checks were abolished and special stages were introduced in 1961.

Handicaps, however, were more difficult to kill off. In the 1950s and 1960s not only were there 'Factors of Comparison' which involved a car's engine size, its homologation group, and even its weight, but there was even one attempt to govern a car's performance by the number of tyres used. It was not until 1968 that the first-ever 'scratch' event was held.

By the 1950s the more serious crews always practised the route before the event, and by the mid-1960s 'ice-notes' crews had been added to a team's efforts. Tyre choice doubled, re-doubled, and became almost ludicrously complex as the 1970s progressed. By the 1980s the Monte Carlo rally was as much of a megabuck, high-technology, exercise as any other in the World Championship calendar – with the weather as an added problem to be faced by a team's planners.

Except on the occasions when the rally organisers have apparently tried to commit collective suicide (the fiascos over the Panhard-favouring 'weight-handicap' of 1961, the hounding of the British BMC

and Ford teams over 'illegal' headlamps in 1966, and the mass disqualification of crews in 1973 were three perfect examples) the event has always retained its charm.

In the 1990s, as on so many other occasions, the best drivers in the world will take the best rally cars in the world, to battle with the wintry conditions. There will be great performances – and disappointments. There will be dramas – and farce. There will be blizzard years – and dry years.

Even so, there will always be a Monte. See you on the Turini?

Origins

Modest beginnings

The original Monte Carlo rally of 1911 was a very modest little affair. That Societé des Bains de Mer, at Monaco, apparently decided that since there was virtually no tourist business in Monte Carlo at the beginning of each year, and since well-to-do sportsmen were turning to motor cars in large numbers, they should organise a rally to satisfy both trends.

Late in 1910 Anthony Noghes, President of the Automobile and Cycle Club of Monaco, announced that there would be a rally to Monte Carlo in January 1911. It was to be open to absolutely any type of motor car. There was no tight timing – competitors could choose their own time of starting, and were allowed seven days to reach the Principality. In many cases it was not the owners but the owners' chauffeurs who did the driving!

No-one from Britain was involved, and Britain's 'establishment' motoring magazine, *The Autocar*, was rather sniffy about the whole business in its issue dated January 21st, 1911:

'Twenty-three entries have been received for what the French press designate *Le Rallye International de Monaco*. As far as we can ascertain, this is in the nature of a "go-as-you-

please" competition for motorists starting from such divergent points of the Continent as Paris, Geneva, Boulogne-sur-Mer, Vienna, Brussels and Berlin... All are to meet at Monaco on the 28th inst., where a *fête* will be held....'

Prizes took account of speed, distance, the number of persons carried, the comfort of the car, and its state on arrival. Journey lengths varied considerably (the longest was 1,055 miles from Berlin), but the low target average speed of 15½ m.p.h. allowed everyone time for rest, refreshment – and enjoyment.

Most crews – 12 out of 23 which entered – elected to start from Paris, and the winner was adjudged to be Henri Rougier on a 25 h.p. Turcat Mery, who completed a wintry 570 miles in only 28 hours 1 min. and 7 sec., averaging more than 20 m.p.h. Not only was Rougier given several magnificent trophies, but a first prize equivalent to £400, a *very* large sum indeed in the currency of the day.

The dubious honour of making the Monte Carlo rally's first protest went to Captain Von Esmach, who had started from Berlin. He declined to accept an award for finishing sixth, presumably because he thought he would have finished higher if he had not been held up by French customs officials....

1911

The first-ever Monte Carlo rally. Starting points from Berlin, Boulogne, Brussels, Geneva, Paris, Vienna: no common route.

1.	Rougier	(Turcat Mery)	Paris
2.	Aspaigu	(Gobron)	
3.	Beutler	(Martini)	
4.	Demoncoau	(Gobron)	
5.	Testa	(Motobloc)	
6.	Goldstick	(La Buer)	

[Capt. Von Eismach refused to accept sixth place...]

23 entries, 20 starters

1912

The Monte Carlo authorities, though not overwhelmed by the small entry, or by the lack of publicity the event received outside France, decided to have another go, and duly arranged for a second event to be held in January, 1912.

This time there seemed to be a lot more interest, for no fewer than 87 competitors decided to take part, though only 60 actually started, one of them from St. Petersburg (a city renamed since then – it is now Leningrad) in Russia.

The formula was the same, and the required average speed of 15½ m.p.h. was still the same, but there was an even wider selection of starting points than before. Thirty-one crews started from Paris, but others started from Vienna, Berlin, Geneva, Brussels, Le Havre, Amsterdam, Boulogne, Turin and St. Petersburg. Clearly the organisers had been hoping to tempt British drivers to cross the Channel and start from a port (Boulogne in both years, Le Havre in 1912), but there was no response.

Even though the cars, by modern standards, were primitive, and snow chains were neither reliable nor universally used, some of the average speeds attained were quite amazing. Denoncin's 40 h.p. Gobron took only 24 hours 41 min. to drive from Paris – breakfast time to breakfast time – while Chalet's Schneider averaged 31 m.p.h. over the by-no-means easy 416-mile journey from Geneva.

In those days, by the way, rallying was still for gentlemen, so controls and checks were only open during the daytime – if a competitor arrived after a control had closed for the night, he was obliged to wait around until the following morning, which did nothing for his average speed!

On this occasion, and after a great deal of argument over the allocation of 'comfort' marks, Monsieur Beutler (who had started from Berlin in a Berliet) was acclaimed the victor. He had averaged a mere 18 miles an hour, but had clearly made up for this in other departments. In 1912, as in later years, the organisers were not willing to unveil their judging methods, nor to modify them in the light of reasonable protests!

*Starting points from Amsterdam, Berlin, Boulogne, Brussels, Geneva,
Le Havre, Paris, St. Petersburg, Turin, Vienna: no common route*

1.   Beutler   (Berliet) Berlin
2.   Von Eismark   (Dunkop)
3.   Meuiner   (Delaunay Belleville)
4.   Serra   (Rolls-Royce)
5.   Fischer   (Mercedes)
6.   Bercy   (Metallurgique)

87 entries, 60 starters

1913 — 1923

After the 1912 event, there was so little pressure for another Monte Carlo to be held that it was not promoted in 1913 and 1914. Even though the Principality was not involved in the First World War of 1914–1918, this put a stop to all motor sport for several years. Politically, things got back to normal by 1920, but it was not until 1924 that the organisers tried again. . . .

Highlights of the modern Monte

The Eighties brought the four wheel drive revolution, starting with the Quattro (opposite). The lower photograph shows Mikkola on the model's first appearance in 1981 while the upper photograph shows Rohrl completing a personal hattrick in 1984. The Supercar generation lasted until 1986: the spread on pages 18 and 19 shows Toivonen winning for the last time in the Lancia. Tragically, his subsequent death helped bring about the switch to less highly modified Group A cars. The first Group A year, 1987, brought victory for Biasion's Lancia, as depicted in the lower photograph on page 24. What a contrast to Rohrl's Lancia Rally, winner in 1983, pictured in the photo above. Rohrl first won in 1980 in a Fiat: that success is depicted in the lower photograph on page 21. He won next in 1982 with Opel. That triumph is depicted in the lower photographs on page 20. Above, on pages 20 and 21, are scenes from Vatanen's 1985 win: Victory for the Peugeot 205. Small cars have long been effective on the Monte, and another famous victory was that of Ragnotti, winner in 1981 in a Renault 5 and depicted in the spread on pages 22 and 23.

Part 1: Struggling against the elements

The only 'spring-time' Monte

The Great War of 1914–1918 changed everything. Not only did it slaughter millions of men, but it also brought the economies of many countries, notably France, to their knees. Before the War, Europe had been a prosperous and a relatively free continent. After the War, you needed passports and visas to move around. It was no wonder that the War had been over for five years before the Automobile Club revived the rally.

For 1924, there were no established traditions on which to build. It was 12 years since the last Monte Carlo rally had been held, the motoring magazines of Europe were no more interested than they had ever been. If ever this was going to become an established event, it was going to be a long, uphill slog.

Compared with 1911 and 1912, there was one major change which the organisers came to regret. On this occasion it was decided to run the rally as an integral part of 'Monte Carlo Week', which was timed for mid-March, this festival not only including the rally itself, but the Mont Agel hillclimb on March 16th. The event, in other words, was likely to be a much easier one to complete – yet the organisers only raised the top average speed to 30 k.p.h./18.6 m.p.h. Perhaps it was plain bad luck that

the prestigious Paris-Nice Trial was held in the previous week?

Even though one of the starting points was Glasgow (the first time a British city had been chosen), and the winning car elected to start from Glasgow, the 1924 rally was virtually ignored by the British motoring press.

The Autocar reported on the 2 litre Bignan which M. Ledure proposed to drive from Glasgow, via Folkestone-Boulogne, then through Paris, Lyons, Avignon and Nice to Monte Carlo. The stately six-seater saloon car's specification included chains for the tyres in case of snow, provision for a second dynamo in case it was needed, an automatic windscreen wiper *and* two hand-operated wipers. The Bignan carried a crew of four which, under the complex regulations, gave it a more favourable rating than other, less heavily loaded, cars.

Unhappily, neither *The Autocar* nor *The Motor* reported its passing, nor carried results. Authoritative French magazines such as *La Vie Automobile* also ignored the rally – it was a real miracle that it survived, to go on to greater things.

For all these reasons, we know very little about the 1924 Monte, which is tragic when one considers that it was the original ancestor of a famous series of between-wars events.

We do know, however, that the choice of a March date was misguided, and that the event was a flop. Would things be better in 1925?

1924

Third rally, held after a 12-year gap, and on this occasion run in March. The first Monte with a British (Glasgow) starting point.

1. Ledure (Bignan) Glasgow
2. de Marquet (Metallurgique)
3. Barbillon (Bignan)

Back to the 'traditional' January date

As in 1912, so in 1925, the second Monte in the series was more successful than the first. Not only was there a respectable entry of 48 cars, but the event was moved back to a January date, thus re-establishing the traditional period over which the world's most famous rally is held.

Thirty-two competitors actually reached Monte Carlo, from a variety of starting points which included Tunis in North Africa. Two crews chose to start from Glasgow – one being the Hon. Victor Bruce in a two-seater AC (fitted with an advanced six-cylinder overhead camshaft engine), the other being Van Roggen's 1.1 litre Imperia, which was fitted with a four-seater saloon car body. The AC left Glasgow at 2.30 p.m. on the Monday, when the Imperia was long gone, for it had started at 11.18 p.m. on the Sunday evening!

The AC's British route was via Manchester, London and Folkestone, by ship to Boulogne, and on to Paris, Lyons and Avignon before reaching Monte Carlo. This saga occupied 1,222 miles, and was scheduled to last 65 hours.

Every car which reached Monte Carlo had to tackle the Mont des Mules hill climb, and a 50-mile reliability trial, this including the La Turbie road and the Col de Braus, both of which would soon become traditional Monte Carlo rally sections.

Several other traditions were established in 1925. One was that those competitors travelling the furthest to the Principality would gain most credit marks – which meant that M. F. Repusseau, who started his 40 h.p. Renault from Tunis and drove by way of Tangier, a ferry crossing to Spain, and then travelled up through Madrid and San Sebastian, always had an advantage, for the distance covered was no less than 2,400 miles.

The other innovation was that the elegance and comfort competition, once an integral part of the main event, was now separately held at the close of the road section – on this occasion M. Hepner's Armstrong Siddeley won the 'closed car' award, while a Panhard-Levassor triumphed in the open car category.

Mont des Mules is a three kilometre climb, where fastest time was set by Mme. Mertens' Lancia Lambda in 3 min. 55.2 sec. – with no other car – not even Goldstuck's large Hispano-Suiza – beating the four-minute barrier. Then, as so often in later years, Lancia was an outstanding marque in this famous event.

In the regularity trial, competitors were asked to average the same speed as they had achieved on their individual runs to Monte Carlo. All would have been well for the gargantuan Renault, except that it had enormous difficulty in getting round the tight hairpin bends – *The Autocar* report assures us that it had to be reversed on 39 occasions.

In the end, therefore, the Renault only beat Madame Mertens' more nimble Lancia Lambda sports car (which had also started from Tunis) by five marks. The intrepid lady had travelled all the way with only her husband for company. It was, and still is, the highest place ever achieved in the Monte Carlo rally by a lady driver. Not even Pat Moss, or Michele Mouton, could come so close in the modern era.

1925

Event once again held in January: two starters from Glasgow, two British starters

1. M. Repusseau   (Renault 40hp) Tunis
2. Mme. Mertens   (Lancia Lambda)
3. Lt. Lamarche   (F.N.)
4. M. Blanc   (De Dion)
5. Williams   (Hispano-Suiza)

48 entries, 32 finishers

1926

The first British victory

Once again this, the pioneering winter rally, was improved and made even tougher than before. The maximum permitted average speed rose to 35 k.p.h./22 m.p.h. and, as before, there was a complex marking system which encouraged competitors to drive rapidly over very long distances.

Although there were 18 starting points, those trying for outright victory chose far-flung points to begin their epic journey. As *La Vie Automobile* recounted, each extra kilometre over the first thousand was worth 0.015 points, and each extra k.p.h. on the achieved average speed was worth five points. Bonus points were also awarded for the number of passengers carried, this bonus depending on the engine size of the car used!

There was more. As in 1925 there was also to be a speed and regularity test, taking in the La Turbie road and the Col de Braus, where competitors were asked to average the same as they had achieved on the run down to Monte Carlo.

Complicated? Maybe – but it also established the complexity which was set to continue all the way to the 1960s. The miracle was that so many competitors continued to pit themselves, not only against the winter and the clock, but against the byzantine minds of the rally organisers.

There was just one British competitor – the Hon. Victor Bruce – co-driven by the photographer W. J. Brunell, and using a 2 litre AC tourer, actually a different car from that which he had used in 1925. He chose to start from John O'Groats, an epic trip totalling 2,461km/1,529 miles, and opted for the maximum allowable speed – this being *after* he had driven all the way up from London to the northern tip of Scotland to start the event! This was not merely a holiday trip to the Mediterranean, but a serious attempt to win the event.

Other routes varied between the gentle 417-mile run from Geneva, to the 1,435-mile trek from Gibraltar. This, however, was by no means the longest distance covered. M. E. P. Malaret effectively started his event from Paris, drove to Marseilles, shipped his car to Tunis, then joined in with other competitors, drove to Tangier, then shipped the car to Gibraltar, and passed through San Sebastian on his way to Monte Carlo!

Although Tunis was a favourite starting spot (and surely one could rely on the weather in North Africa?), it turned into a nightmare for the crews who chose it. Once over the Straits of Gibraltar, they encountered snow-storms in the mountains and heavy flooding in the valleys. Malaret's car ruined its engine in one of those floods, which left the Hon. Victor Bruce's AC in the clear. All in all, nearly half the 45 starters dropped out before reaching Monte Carlo.

When he arrived, unscathed, in Monte Carlo, after several alarums which included digging through snowdrifts in the Scottish Highlands, and almost missing the cross-Channel boat, the AC driver was tied for first place with M. Bussienne's Sizaire-Frères, which had started from Brest, but had covered only 870 miles.

It was all down to the last, twisty, mountainous and snowy loop behind the Principality, in which the AC comprehensively defeated the Sizaire-Frères. Once again a lady – Madame Marika (who was the wife of a Citroën dealer) – finished well up the field, and everyone seemed to agree that this was a tough test for crew and machine.

1926

The first year in which a British team won: 18 starting points: no common route

1. Hon. V. Bruce/W. J. Brunell *(AC) John O'Groats*
2. Bussienne *(Sizaire-Frères)*
3. Mme. Marika *(Citroën)*
4. Veishlai *(Chrysler)*
5. Williams *(Hispano-Suiza)*
6. Monthier *(Peugeot)*

45 starters, 24 finishers

A real test of endurance

By this time the rally had settled down into a pattern. Not only was it a winter event, with speed and regularity tests at the finish to sort out a result, but there was a complex marking formula to sort out the *real* drivers from the dilettantes.

Consider this – if you decided to enter the rally in 1927, you had to take account of the 'handicap' on distance covered, the average speed you would choose to run, and the number of passengers you would take along for the ride; the last figure varied depending on the engine size of the chosen car.

In 1927, too, there was a further complication, for the average speed target over the now-traditional Col de Braus circuit was to vary from class to class – a 1.1 litre car was asked to average 30 k.p.h./18.6 m.p.h., whereas a car with an engine larger than 2.0 litres had to average 34 k.p.h./21.1 m.p.h.

Overall, however, it chose to pick a starting point which was as far away from Monte Carlo as possible. Victor Bruce's famous victory in 1926 had been assured when he chose the 1,529-mile run in from John O'Groats (and made it through, without penalty) – but in 1927 this was not likely to be enough. Not only was there to be a starting point from Konigsberg (now renamed Kalingrad) in Eastern Prussia (eight crews chose to tackle this

1,638-mile journey), but there was even the 1,840-mile marathon from Stockholm, and the 1,927-mile epic from Bucharest, the capital of Rumania.

None of these January journeys would be easy, even today, but more than 60 years ago they set challenges which could only be met by motoring heroes. Some crews still chose to use tourers with, at best, rather draughty 'all-weather' equipment. There was no such thing as an in-car heater, and the grip from narrow 'vintage' tyres was almost non-existent on snow and ice.

Following the Hon. Victor Bruce's 1926 win there was a little more British interest – but not much. Two ACs were entered – one from John O'Groats for Mrs. V. A. Bruce, whose famous husband accompanied her in the four-door saloon type chosen for that year's event, and one from Glasgow for Cecil May. Captain Francis Samuelson started from Doncaster in a two-seater, 750cc Ratier, while J. R. Cox started from London in a Fiat.

Interest in the event, in fact, was rising rapidly, for there was a much enlarged entry of 65 cars, although only 52 of them actually started the event. One team had attempted to beat all distance records by electing to start from Athens, but as on so many occasions in the inter-war years the roads through the Balkans were quite impassable in winter.

Those who chose to start from Gibraltar faced identical hazards to those of January 1926 – snow at height, and floods on the plains – so all were badly handicapped. Those who chose to cram their saloon cars full of passengers had an uncomfortable time, but gained several bonus points per passenger – six for a 1.1 litre car, shading down to only three points for cars larger than 2.0 litres.

The Autocar's enthusiastic report (how different this was from its original attitude in 1911!) also made it clear that many teams were planning to spend nights in bed:

'... competitors starting from Koenigsberg, in Eastern Prussia, were limited to 76 hours if they wished to reach the maximum average. Estimating 14 hours a day *actual running* [the italics are mine] the average speed works out at 36 m.p.h., and to maintain such an average it would be necessary to keep the car going at 45 to 50 m.p.h. for long distances...'

For many competitors, however, there was a fairly comfortable, if cold, run down to Monte Carlo, where those who had driven the longest distances were immediately placed at the head of the field. There was an optional hillclimb of Mont des Mules, which had no bearing on the results of the rally – with Lt. Lamarche's 1.5 litre F.N. setting FTD in 3 min. 51.2 sec.

The keenest competitors had already started carrying out pre-rally reconnaissance over the Col de Braus – some even placing markers along the roadside at what, for them, were three-minute intervals. This was a ploy soon ruined by spectators (or, whisper it, by other competitors?), who moved some of the poles!

Lefebre's supercharged 1.1 litre Amilcar was a comfortable winner on this occasion, not only having driven in from Koenigsberg, beating two other Koenigsberg starters into second and third places, but having a 5.3 point margin over any rival.

1927

Many different starting points, including Konigsberg, John O'Groats, Bucharest, Gibraltar: no common route before arrival

1.	Lefebre	(Amilcar 1100)	Konigsberg
2.	Clausse	(Celtic-Bignani)	
3.	Bussienne	(Sizaire-Frères)	
4.	Lt. Lamarche	(F.N.)	
5.	Prince Racovitza	(Steyr)	
6.	Mrs. V. A. Bruce	(AC)	

65 entries, 52 starters, 45 finishers

Another endurance victory

The rally was now becoming very fashionable, for entries rose yet again for 1928. There had been 45 starters in 1926, 52 in 1927, but no fewer than 78 crews entered for the 1928 event. The British motoring press, at last, sat up and took proper notice, with *The Autocar* publishing a detailed guide, a two-page interim story, and a full four-page report of the event itself. Famous sports editor S.C.H. 'Sammy' Davis went along, as a passenger, in A.H. Pass's 20 h.p. six-cylinder Weymann-bodied Sunbeam.

The event was still being refined, rather than being changed considerably from year to year. On this occasion the number of far-flung starting points was reduced to eleven, though less dedicated competitors could (and did) join in at intermediate controls along the way.

The points scoring system almost ensured that the winning car would have travelled the maximum possible distance, and would have a small engine. This meant that the John O'Groats start, although creditable, was not likely to entertain the winner, for it was 'only' 1,528 miles from the Mediterranean. Stockholm, on the other hand, was 1,843 miles (and was chosen, on this occasion, by Mrs Bruce), and the most demanding routes of all were those from Bucharest (1,927 miles, but with a very dodgy

weather record), from Constantinople, and from Salonika, all of which faced harrowing battles to get through the Balkans to Northern Italy.

Forty-three of the 78 cars entered were French, whereas 11 were British, nine German/Austrian, five American and two Belgian. Nine cars, six of them British, chose to start from John O'Groats and, as ever, the assistant secretary of the Royal Scottish Automobile Club, A.K. Stevenson, journeyed to the tip of Scotland to act as official starter, hitching a lift from A.H. Pass's Sunbeam to ease the journey. The problem, for these crews, was actually to reach the start – W.J. Brunell discovered that he had to dig his way through the Grampians, to blaze a trail for the others.

The John O'Groats starters, in fact, began their journey before dawn on the Sunday, yet arrived in London at about 8 a.m. the following day. After a channel crossing the cars were then routed through Paris, to arrive in Monte Carlo itself on the Wednesday afternoon. At the optimum average speed (still 35 k.p.h./21.7 m.p.h.) this meant an overall journey time of 70 hr. 24 min. As 'Sammy' Davis also pointed out, a competitor was also '... allowed the time of his passage if he has a sea crossing, one hour for embarkation, one hour for landing, and one hour for crossing a frontier. Crossing by the Folkestone-Boulogne route gives 1 hr. 20 min. plus three more hours, so if he wishes to time his arrival at Monte Carlo for 10 a.m. on Wednesday he must leave John O'Groats 74 hr. 40 min. earlier... The organisers are not concerned with whatever speed a driver may choose to make between the controls through which he must pass on his journey, in this case Glasgow, Doncaster, London, Paris, Lyons and Avignon, except that the affair is not a race...'

Even before the surviving cars tacked the *Concours de Regularité* – the well-established 83 km./52 mile circuit behind Monte Carlo – the results had virtually been settled. Jacques Bignan (in his 9 h.p. Fiat Type 509) and three other drivers struggled through from Bucharest, Mrs. Bruce survived an ice-bound journey from Stockholm, while seven crews also made it from Koenigsberg – which meant they were almost ensured of top placings, for theirs were the longest journeys, attracting the most bonus marks.

The Col de Braus circuit included three control points, with strict regularity required. Most crews found time to make a trial run or two on the day before the test itself (at a 34 k.p.h./21 m.p.h. average, the loop occupied less than three hours), and found little snow and ice on this occasion.

In the end, however, Bignan's gallant little Fiat won the event, but it was more accurate to state that Bucharest beat Koenigsberg, from Bucharest, Stockholm and Koenigsberg respectively.

1928

Starting points from Athens, Brest, Bucharest, Constantinople, Gibraltar, John O'Groats, Koenigsberg, Oslo, Palermo, Stockholm, Trieste, and intermediate towns along the way: no common route.

1.	J. Bignan	(Fiat Type 509, 9 h.p.)	Bucharest
2.	Malaret	(Fiat)	
3.	Ms. Versigny	(Talbot)	
4.	P. Bussienne	(Sizaire-Frères)	
5.	Hon. Mrs. V. Bruce	(AC)	
6.	Holzknecht	(Steyr)	

78 entries, 59 starters, 47 finishers

Severe weather decimates the field

The rally's reputation advanced even further in 1929. Not only was there a record entry – 84 cars actually started – but the weather was truly wintry, and gave glamour to the stories told by the 24 cars which survived. There was also a notable 'first' outright victory for an American car. Dr. Van Eijk's Graham-Paige, made in Detroit, was surely more at home in the city streets of North America than the mountains of Europe?

In one way the organisers regressed, for they allowed competitors to start their journeys to the sunshine from no fewer than 27 different towns or cities. Some of these – London, Brussels, Lyons and Frankfurt, for example – were merely intermediate points visited by the cars which had started from more remote locations.

As before, for the serious competitors rally distance was everything, and these seemed to be increasing every year. The longest journey of all was theoretically that from Athens (2,291 miles), which overshadowed every other route, through Lwow in Poland (1,856), Riga on the Baltic (1,834 miles) and Stockholm (1,840 miles) all set their own challenges.

The conundrum here was that the road from Athens was forecast to be snow-bound, so the four crews who chose this glamorous spot were not

guaranteed a high placing. Only three cars chose Stockholm (but one of these was eventually judged the winner), six chose Lwow, and 20 chose Riga.

Mrs. Bruce and Victor Leverett chose the start from Riga, as did a balding bundle of energy called Donald Healey who on this occasion drove a Triumph Super Seven. John O'Groats, at 'only' 1,529 miles, attracted 14 entries, though only 12 of them actually took the start.

On this occasion, the competition was made more severe. The top average speed required on the concentration run had been raised to 40 k.p.h./24.8 m.p.h., and after arrival in Monte Carlo there was to be a double circuit of the Col de Braus loop, instead of the single loop which had been used since 1925.

Right from the start, it was clear that this would be no ordinary Monte Carlo rally, for there was a lot of snow all over Europe. Of the 12 cars which started from John O'Groats, only five caught the Dover cross-channel ferry on time. Those trying to get to Riga even to start the rally found it well-nigh impossible. Both Donald Healey and Mrs. Bruce cut their losses (and their chances of a good place in the rally) by electing to start from Berlin instead.

It was the same story, all over Europe, for if there was no snow and ice, there was dense fog, and car

In 1929 the Monte Carlo rally was still a great adventure. This Talbot, running as Car No. 1, was driven by Miss Kitty Brunell, and started from John O'Groats. In those days there were no studded tyres, and no heaters either!

after car simply disappeared. For the hours when a crawl was needed, the crews could only make up time in clear visibility by running at 60 or 70 m.p.h. One statistic tells its own story – 60 of the 84 cars which started the rally – 71 per cent of them – retired, or arrived too late to be classified. Donald Healey's story was the most heart-breaking of all – well up to time at Frejus, close to Nice, his little Triumph was then delayed on the twisty Corniche towards Monte Carlo, and was excluded by just two minutes.

The eventual winner, Dr. van Eijk, started out from Stockholm with three passengers, having been warned that the roads were impassable. From Sweden to Germany three ferries had to be used, one of which had already left its berth, but was called back to keep him in the event. At one point he went off the road in a snowstorm, and horses were needed to tug the damaged car back on to the road, and he needed to get his damaged car repaired in Holland, on the way through.

A look at the finishing list shows that all cars from some starting points – Athens, Lwow and Riga

among them – were completely eliminated. The 'long-distance' crews who survived came from Stockholm, Bucharest, Gibraltar and Warsaw.

In an event as severe as this, the two-loop regularity test was almost, but not quite, a formality. There were eight secret checks, but it was a crash on an early bend which eliminated Victor Szmick's 875cc Weiss-Manfred, which had struggled through from Bucharest to lead the rally on arrival. Even Dr. van Eijk's car suffered gearbox problems and clocked in late at one point.

Competitors who survived the double journey, to and from John O'Groats, were heard to say 'never again', but for those who fought their way down through France in the fog, conditions must have been even worse.

The organisers were delighted – this was *exactly* what they wanted to nurture, the event's reputation as a real 'killer'. Could it possibly be as bad in 1930?

Kitty Brunell, once again, was 'Ladies First' in the 1930 event, running No. 1 in her Talbot; this was a wintry scene near Castillon, not far north of Monte Carlo...

Between the wars, and until the early 1950s, the Concours de Confort *was an important part of the Monte. This was 1929 and, as ever it seemed, the Mediterranean sun made it all seem worthwhile.*

1929

Starting points from 27 different places, principally from Bucharest, John O'Groats, Lwow, Riga, Stockholm, Warsaw: no common route.

1. *Dr. Sprenger van Eijk*   *(Graham Paige) Stockholm*
2. *Szmick*   *(Weiss-Manfred)*
3. *Visser*   *(Lancia)*
4. *Morillon*   *(Peugeot)*
5. *A. Berlesco*   *(Citröen)*
6. *H. Petit*   *(Licorne)*

93 entries, 84 starters, 24 finishers

More competitors, in an 'easy' year

The epic nature of the 1929 had a marvellous effect on public opinion. Not only did the newspapers begin to talk of the rally as the world's most difficult motoring event, but competitors positively flocked to take part. In January 1930, no fewer than 115 comprehensively-equipped cars started this, the ninth Monte Carlo rally.

Unfortunately for sensation seekers, the weatherman did not provide blizzard conditions like those which had existed in 1929. The 1930 rally, indeed, goes down in history as something of an 'easy' year, for 88 of the starters made it to Monte Carlo, to take part in the hillclimb, the regularity test, the Concours, the glittering celebration ball, and the prize-giving, all of which ensured that competitors stayed in the packed Principality for at least four days. Furthermore, some cars arrived at the Monte Carlo arrival control three hours before it was due to open, and no fewer than 70 crews gained maximum possible points for keeping the highest authorised average speeds.

Once again there was a wide choice of starting points — those furthest from Monte Carlo, usually with the most difficult and demanding roads in between, being those chosen by serious competitors. A look down the list showed several old favourites –

Athens, Bucharest and Gibralter – and the new ones included Jassy in Rumania (2,186 miles from Monte Carlo), and Tallinn in Estonia (even further away from the Mediterranean than Riga had been in 1929, at 2,159 miles). Sundsvall, north of Sweden, was 2,128 miles away.

John O'Groats starters now travelled by way of Nantes, on the Bay of Biscay, to reach Lyons, so their distance was increased to 1,837 miles. Twenty-six crews, almost all British, and all but seven in British cars, chose this route. From John O'Groats, the route led through controls at Glasgow, Doncaster and London, and – as ever – it was essential to catch the afternoon boat from Folkestone to Boulogne, or fall completely out of the running. Even so, if cars could get through from Athens, Jassy or Tallinn, they were favourite to do well.

Some of the 'names' in the list were becoming more recognisable, for in addition to Donald Healey, E.P. Malaret, Jacques Bignan and Dr. van Eijk, there were entries for racing drivers Rudolph Caracciola, Boris Ivanovsky and Glen Kidston. Beforehand, a lot of tactical entries had been made, with distance weighed against possible mild weather – Bignan and Dr. van Eijk chose Jassy, while Donald Healey (Triumph Super Seven), Malaret and Carac-

41

ciola all chose Tallinn. Mrs. Bruce chose to trek to Sundsvall in Northern Sweden, even though there were three chancy ferry trips spanning Sweden and Denmark to be tackled on the run south.

Immediately before the 'off' the weather was suspiciously spring-like, with fog forecast for the Rhône Valley, and snow on high ground between Roanne and Lyons.

On the way from John O'Groats to Glasgow, Kidston crashed his 'blower' Bentley, and Capt. J.E.P. Howey went off at the same spot in his Mercedes-Benz sports car. Repairs were hastily made to badly bent cars, but both were effectively out of the running in the first few hours.

Most crews reported an easy run, especially compared with 1930, and for British enthusiasts there was the delight of seeing Healey's tiny Triumph (which could not possibly have had a top speed any higher than 50 m.p.h.!) on time, and in very good shape, after a marathon run from Tallinn, via Riga, Koenigsberg, Berlin, Brussels, Paris and Lyons.

Because the regularity test (two circuits of the Col de Braus loop) was only worth eight points, it could not upset the 'distance' marks gained by the well-rested crews. Nevertheless, it was an interesting motoring, and time-keeping, challenge – to achieve exactly 32 k.p.h./20 m.p.h. over every section of the route, even after much diligent practice. In fact the most accomplished performances were set by the remarkable Healey, a feat equalled by H. Petit in his Licorne. As Petit had started from Jassy, which was 42 km./26 miles further away from Monte Carlo, he won the event.

The importance of 'distance' was emphasised in the results, for all the first six finishers started from Jassy, while the next six crews all started from Tallinn. The gallant Healey was placed seventh, the next highest-placed British driver being Mrs. V.A. Bruce, 21st, starting from Sundsvall.

The *Concours de Confort*, a separate competition organised at the close of the event, was becoming more important – on this occasion the Grand Prix d'Honneur being won by A.H. Pass's Sunbeam.

1930

Starting points from: *Athens, Barcelona, Bucharest, Constantinople, Gibraltar, Jassy, John O'Groats, Lisbon, Oslo, Palermo, Sundsvall, Tallinn, and intermediate points: no common route.*

1. H. Petit (Licorne) Jassy
2. Cdt. Al Berlesco (De Soto)
3. A. Blin D'Orimont (Studebaker)
4. Dr. Sprenger van Eijk (Graham-Paige)
5. J. Bignan (Fiat)
6. Cdt. E. Urdariono (Fiat)

141 entries, 115 starters, 88 finishers

Donald Healey's magnificent Invicta win

Without question, the only way to remember the 1931 rally, is as Donald Healey's Monte. After struggling against the odds – weather *and* restricted car performance – for a couple of years, the redoubtable Cornishman got his hands on a 4½ litre low-chassis Invicta and won the event outright.

Today's equivalent would have been to use a Mini for two years, then arrange to borrow a 'works' Ford Sierra RS Cosworth for a third occasion. The difference – in performance, and in car 'image' – was just as stark.

Once again the Automobile Club attracted a record entry – this time of 156 cars, three times as many as in 1926, just five years earlier. There seemed to be no limit to the event's potential, even if it was, and would remain, something of a lottery. At least the favourable handicap for cramming the car full of passengers was merely an incredible memory from the past.

For 1931 many of the routes were almost exactly like those of 1930, which is to say that there were long treks originating in Athens, Jassy, Tallinn and Sundsvall. However, on this occasion there was also a 2,261 mile challenge from Stavanger in Norway (which was chosen by many of the serious crews), and a projected starting point from Land's End which was chosen by no-one at all!

One often forgets, incidentally, that some competitors – such as Louis Chiron, who travelled from Monte Carlo to Stavanger to start the rally – often completed at least 1,000 miles before the competition even began.

Forty-five crews, no less, elected to start from Stavanger, which had a longer 'Start – Monte Carlo' distance than any except Athens, while there were 14 cars from Jassy, and nine from Tallinn. In spite of the fact that no-one choosing this point could possibly win, there were 23 crews electing to start from John O'Groats. In previous years, no crew had ever got through from Athens, which explains its lack of popularity.

For the first time in years, there were changes to the format of the event. On the long road sections the minimum average speed for smaller cars was now 35 k.p.h./21.7 m.p.h., while that for larger cars was 40 k.p.h./24.9 m.p.h. Then, on arrival in Monte Carlo, those cars which had covered the greatest distances were faced with an acceleration and braking test in the centre of the Principality. The Col de Braus regularity test had been abandoned – but it would be back in the future.

For the British contingent, weather conditions

were worse than in 1930, with a blizzard raging in the Grampians, though 16 of the 21 starters eventually turned up at Folkestone, one of them (Grant's Talbot) needing a new front axle after a crash in south London.

British crews making for the Stavanger start had difficulty even in getting to that Norwegian town, for the North Sea ferry boat docked 11 hours late at Bergen, though everyone faced the starter's flag in due course.

The Athens contingent, 14 strong in the entry list, was reduced to seven even before the start when several crews could not even get into Greece; one who had to abandon, no less, was Robert Senechal, in an eight-cylinder Delage. Well before the column reached France, all but the celebrated Jacques Bignan had dropped out, but the burly and quite imperturbable Frenchman turned up in Monte Carlo, the very first Monte competitor ever to complete the run from Athens.

Soon it became obvious that survivors from Stavanger would win the event – in fact every car in the top ten started from the Norwegian locality. None of those who chose Lwow achieved anything, while only one crew of the nine which had nominated Tallinn as a starting point actually made it to the start. Two cars came through from Lwow, none at all from Tallinn.

As *The Autocar* stated in its report:

'At the start of the acceleration and braking tests practically all the cars from Stavanger were equal, and the winner was looked for among Invicta, Lagonda, Bugatti and Lorraine. The best aggregate performance, however, was that of D.M. Healey's open sports Invicta...'

But not quite the best performance of the whole entry. The Invicta's time, was fastest of all in the 250 metre acceleration test, but was beaten, overall, by T.C. Mann's Lagonda. Unfortunately for Mr. Mann, he had chosen to start from Glasgow, which left him nowhere in the overall classification.

The Invicta's fabulous success, however, was not achieved without a panic. After the event Donald Healey revealed that he had been involved in a road accident in Norway, hitting a telegraph pole, the back axle had been pushed 1½ inches off centre, and for the rest of the event the car had proceeded crabwise, with braking and steering both badly affected!

1931

Starting points from: Athens, Gibraltar, Jassy, John O'Groats, Lisbon, Palermo, Stavanger, Tallinn, and many other intermediate points: no common route

1.   D.M. Healey   *(Invicta 4½ litre) Stavanger*
2.   J.P. Wimille   *(Lorraine)*
3.   L. Schell   *(Bugatti)*
4.   Lord de Clifford   *(Lagonda)*
5.   J. Sprenger van Eijk   *(Graham)*
6.   M. Schaar   *(Chrysler)*

156 entries, 149 starters, 62 finishers

Winning by driving at 1½ m.p.h.

New ground was broken, in several ways, in 1932. Not only was a new starting point – Umea – chosen by all the top cars, but this was the first of what many historians call the 'Hotchkiss years'. Unhappily the effects of the world Depression were all around, which meant that there was not as much money to spare on winter holidays, and the entry was well down on the previous (record) year.

As S.C.H. 'Sammy' Davis wrote in his preview: 'Remember, first of all, that the main object of a competitor is to cover the longest distance possible, and that if one group of competitors arrives in Monte Carlo from a certain starting place, all that group automatically takes precedence over any other group...'

In 1932 this meant that a newly-chosen starting point, Umea in northern Sweden, was automatically going to be very popular, for it was 2,331 miles from Monte Carlo. Athens was actually 21 miles further away but no-one had yet managed to force his way through Yugoslavia in the snows of January. (Jacques Bignan actually made it in 1931, but was outside time limits).

Accordingly, more than 50 crews – half the entry – chose Umea, some flogging many hundreds of miles from their homes to get to the town, located on the Gulf of Bothnia, on Sweden's east coast. Notable among the Umea runners were 1932 winner Donald Healey (once again Invicta-mounted), Louis Chiron, journalist Humfrey Symons – and M. Vasselle in a 3½ litre six-cylinder Hotchkiss saloon. Eight crews (including Rupert Riley, driving a Riley) chose Athens, but the popularity of Jassy had plummeted, with only two crews electing to begin their rally there. In the event, every car in the top 18 places had started from Umea.

Although those choosing John O'Groats had no chance of success, there were 13 crews scheduled to make the long trip south, through Glasgow, London, Boulogne, Nantes and Lyons, prominent among them being racing driver Chris Staniland. Cyril Whitcroft, T.C. Mann and Norman Black all chose to start from London, as the John O'Groats runners came through, but theirs was not a serious attempt at success.

Rootes PR man Dudley Noble started from Glasgow in a Hillman Wizard 75 which was towing a caravan! Once again, not a serious attempt to win, but as the combination safely fought its way through, it certainly made plenty of headlines for its manufacturers.

Once again there had been a change in the final

1932, and this Ford V-8 (a new model at the time, destined for great things in future years) poses with its four-man crew, led by J. Walters, before leaving the UK for the Riviera. The result? 62nd Overall . . .

test. There was still no regularity test, and after only one year the acceleration and braking test had also been abandoned. On this occasion cars had to be driven as *slowly* as possible, in top gear, over the first 100 metres of a driving test, then as fast as possible (still in top gear) over the next 100 metres, after which they had to be stopped within 40 metres.

It didn't sound very exciting – but it was the only way in which a winner was to be extracted from the 'long-distance' survivors. Historian Michael Frostick reports newspaper headlines such as: 'Farcical test Ruins Monte Carlo Rally', which it did, in more ways than one, for many cars were geared right down with this test in mind – which must have made the run from Umea purgatorial for many. The ever-resourceful Donald Healey carried small spare wheels, specifically to fit to his car immediately before the final test!

Once the event got under way, the Cassandra's warnings were upheld. Conditions in the Balkans, south of Belgrade, were appalling, but for the first time all five cars in the Athens contingent forced their way through. It was not snow, but floods, which mostly held up the John O'Groats starters, while the large Umea contingent had to put up with

black ice, and those three unavoidable ferry crossings; even Vasselle's car went off the road at one stage. Twenty-eight intrepid crews got through from Umea, and were favourites to win the event after the driving test.

Many local garages were used, immediately before the final test, for wheels, or even axle ratios, to be changed – something which the organisers had apparently not considered would happen. Vasselle's Hotchkiss, it seems, did not change a ratio – but had travelled the whole way from Umea with a top speed of only 50 m.p.h.!

Vasselle's car was outstanding in the slow-fast-stop test, taking 2 min. 35.51 sec. to cover the first 100 yards, which equates to 1½ m.p.h. – the engine was reputedly turning over at about 80 or 85 r.p.m. Healey's Invicta, using borrowed wheels, with its tail nearly scraping the ground, dawdled on for 1 min. 54.91 sec., which was good enough to place him second.

It was a crazy way to finish what was supposed to be a serious event, and the organisers were urged to think again for 1933.

Once again a Sunbeam, that driven by Humfrey Symons, won the Concours de Confort.

1932

Starting points from Athens, Frankfurt, Gibraltar, Jassy, John O'Groats, Lisbon, Palermo, Stavanger, Umea, and other intermediate points: no common route

1.	M. Vasselle	(Hotchkiss 3½ litre)	Umea
2.	D. M. Healey	(Invicta 4½ litre)	
3.	B. Ivanovsky	(Ford)	
4.	P. Escher	(Bugatti)	
5.	L. Mathieson	(Citroën)	
6.	M. Chauvierre	(Chenard-Walcker)	

116 entries, 64 finishers

Donald Healey's Invicta, out testing before the 1933 event, showing its excellent ground clearance, and the specially-cut tyre treads.

Advantage Tallinn

In many ways the 1933 Monte was the 'mixture as before', for it saw Vasselle's 3½ litre Hotchkiss repeat its 1932 victory, the whole thing being settled by a driving test on the harbour front at Monte Carlo after the cars reached the finish.

The major differences, though, were that the organisers had listened to all the complaints about the 'slow driving' test of 1932 – and abandoned it – and there had been yet another shuffle of starting points.

As usual, the Monte Carlo rally was going to be settled in favour of those crews who drove the furthest distance on their way to the Mediterranean. In 1932 Umea and Athens had been the furthest-flung spots. For 1933, however, Tallinn, in Estonia, had re-appeared in the lists, and since this offered a longer journey than Umea or Athens it attracted 30 of the entrants.

With Europe gradually pulling out of the great economic Depression, the entry increased once again, and – following so many British successes in previous years – there were no fewer than 51 entries from these islands, 28 crews electing to start from John O'Groats. One of them driven by Lord de Clifford, was actually an old Bentley chassis fitted with a Gardner diesel engine. Apart from Healey,

other well-known British 'names' included Jack Hobbs, Mrs. Vaughan, Humfrey Symons, Ms. Kay Petre, T.V.G. Selby, H.S. Linfield, F.S. Barnes and H.J. Aldington. Among the Europeans was a new name, soon to become more familiar and more famous – Jean Trevoux, in a 3½ litre Hotchkiss.

The RAC was so fired up by this show of enthusiasm that it chartered the cross-channel steamer *Auto-Carrier* for a special trip from Folkestone, and provided route maps and town plans for the entire journey to Monte Carlo.

Compared with 1932, however, the weather was much worse, and there were blizzard conditions all over Europe. Athens starters, as usual, had to dig their way through, while the Tallinn starters would apparently never even have got started if the rally had begun a day later. When a seasoned competitor like Donald Healey (Invicta) is forced to retire, almost dead with cold, it is tough . . .

Yet, amazingly, 71 cars arrived within time limits at Monte Carlo. No fewer than 17 fought their way through from Tallinn, six from Umea, and just three from Stavanger. There was chaos in Eastern Europe, where the entire Jassy, Bucharest, Lwow and Athens columns were wiped out in the blizzard. Nothing – ground clearance, chains on tyres, help from oxen

51

and horses – could clear a way through snowdrifts for these unfortunate crews. The John O'Groats contingent, however, had better luck, for 24 crews arrived safely.

The winner, therefore, was certain to come from the Tallinn contingent, and it would all be settled by the driving test. Fastest time in the acceleration test was set by Vasselle's powerful Hotchkiss, who also brought his car to halt 16 metres after the end of the sprint. Guyot's big Renault was 0.2 seconds slower to accelerate, and one metre quicker to stop, but under the complex formula (there was never a simple formula in the Monte Carlo rally, between the wars …) he lost a further 0.25 points. By such tiny margins was the rally won and lost.

Although the first 14 finishers had all started from Tallinn (Norman Black's Hudson Essex won the 'other' rally in 15th place, starting from Umea) it was a significant result. Messrs. Roualt and Quinlin (third) would figure in several future events, as would Mme. Schell. Lord de Clifford's old Bentley had done amazingly well, not only to finish the road section, but to take fifth place, overall.

For the John O'Groats starters, of course, it hardly seemed to be worth the trouble, for most of the cars all finished in a bunch, between 24th and 40th overall. But spare a thought for the Palermo runners, from Sicily; two crews started, two finished – last and next to last.

1933

Starting points from Athens, Bucharest, John O'Groats, Palermo, Stavanger, Tallinn, Umea, Valencia, and intermediate points: no common route.

1. M. Vasselle   (Hotchkiss 3½ litre) Tallinn
2. R. Guyot   (Renault)
3. Ms. Roualt and M. Quinlin   (Salmson)
4. Ms. L. Schell & L. Schell   (Talbot)
5. Lord de Clifford   (Bentley-Gardner Diesel)
6. R. Bravard   (Amilcar)

129 entries, 120 starters, 71 finishers

1934

A Hotchkiss hat-trick – from Athens!

This was getting predictable. Not only was the rally winner sure to come from the furthest-flung starting point, but it now began to look as if it had to be a French Hotchkiss *Grand Tourisme* machine. Not that the rest of the world seemed to mind too much – with Europe becoming increasingly prosperous once again, there was money and time to spare, so the entry for the Monte Carlo soared to a new record of 161 crews. There was no change to the format of the driving test, which was a simple acceleration and braking test, as in 1933.

On this occasion, and just to enliven proceedings after the *real* rally was over, the organisers arranged for a long and complex 'wiggle-woggle' driving test to be set up on the Quai Albert 1e.

Because there was no change to the 'distance = success' format of the event, the order of priority for starting points had to be with Athens (2,352 miles), though Bucharest (2,344 miles), Umea (2,349 miles), Tallinn (2,347 miles) and Stavanger (2,299 miles) were close; the rest trailed far behind, and were only favoured by the amateurs.

This was reflected in the spread of entries – 25 crews chose Athens, even though the chances of getting through from Greece, in January, were minimal, 16 Bucharest, 23 Umea, 21 Tallinn, and 19 Stavanger. Twenty-five crews also nominated John O'Groats, whose route through France visited Le Mans, Nantes, Bordeaux and Bayonne... Donald Healey and Jack Ridley (in 'works' Triumph Glorias), like Gas and Trevoux, Dr. van Eijk, Jacques Bignan, Humfrey Symons and Mme Schell all chose Athens, gambling that the roads (and the weather) would be more favourable than in previous years.

It was time, the organisers decided, to start toughening up the average speeds required on the road section, so for the last 1,000 km. or so it was decided to impose a 50 k.p.h./31 m.p.h. schedule. This, make no mistake, was a considerable challenge by 1930s standards, especially when we remember that studded tyres were still a quarter-century into the future.

The fact that no fewer than 114 crews reached Monte Carlo within time limits – another all-time Monte Carlo rally record – proves that this was an easier year than most of those previously held. From Athens the problem was not snow, but muddy and near-impassable roads – cars like the 'works' Triumphs, which had been specially equipped with 'Balloon' tyres had an immediate advantage. There had been a thaw in Sweden before the start, which

A trio of Hotchkiss Grand Routier *machines from the 1934. The car in the centre is the winning 3-litre car, crewed by Gas and Trevoux.*

It was always good to reach Monte Carlo in one piece – this Railton crew, led by F. de Ribiero-Ferreira, had just finished fourth overall in 1934, battling their way through from Athens.

Two famous names, taking part in the acceleration and braking test at the end of the 1934 rally – Donald Healey, in a much-modified Triumph Gloria. Along with Tommy Wisdom, the redoubtable little Cornishman finished third on this occasion.

*What, no other traffic? What, no people? This was a desolate scene on the 1934 rally, with a Ford V8 Model 40 leading a
Lagonda M45.*

Lots of interest from spectators in the 1934. The car in the foreground is a 1931 Chevrolet, while the big tourer is a Lagonda M45 4-litre tourer.

meant that Umea crews had quite an easy run south. Even the Tallinn contingent had a better deal this year, though there was a real sensation when it was learned that twice-winner Vasselle had been eliminated.

John O'Groats starters suffered gale force winds, but all were on time in Aberdeen and Glasgow. Some crews were so far ahead of schedule that they had time for a sleep before taking breakfast at the RAC club in Pall Mall. In the event most crews had little difficulty in keeping up with the dreaded 50 k.p.h. schedule in the Esterelles section.

Amazingly, 15 crews got through, almost all of them unpenalised, from Athens, which meant that one of them was almost certain to win the rally. The driving test ensured that a big and powerful car would defeat all the others, so no-one was surprised when the Gas-Trevoux Hotchkiss recorded fastest time and scooped the pool.

Surprisingly, Ferreira's Railton was slightly slower (by 0.17 sec.) than the Hotchkiss, and although it was better in the braking phase it still had to settle for fourth place. Donald Healey's 1.2 litre engined Triumph set an amazing show, being only 1.1 sec. slower than the Hotchkiss over the 100 metre sprint – and the ever-cheerful Cornishman was rewarded with third place overall, and victory in the up-to-1.5 litre category.

The full list of results shows Athens starters in the top 15 positions, with those starting from John O'Groats filling every slot between 62nd and 78th. For the British amateur driver, therefore, was it worth it?

January 1934, and the Casino terrace is well filled with cars taking part in the concours. Posing, maybe – but in the 1930s this was one of the most important aspects of the event.

1934

Main starting points from Athens, Bucharest, John O'Groats, Palmero, Stavanger, Tallinn, Umea and Valencia, with other cars joining in from intermediate points: no common route.

1. Gas/Trevoux (Hotchkiss 3½ litre) Athens
2. Chauvierre (Chenard-Walcker)
3. D. M. Healey (Triumph Gloria)
4. F. d R. Ferreira (Railton)
5. J. W. Whalley (Ford V8)
6. J. van der Heyden (Studebaker)

161 entries, 150 starters, 114 finishers

1935

Wiggle-woggling to victory

From the mid-1930s a gradual change came over the rally. Until this time the Monte had been a straightforward event – a battle between cars and crews, against the weather and Europe's winter roads. Now the cars were becoming more and more specialised, in an attempt to get round whatever handicap, or challenge, the organisers posed. The competitors must have been happy with this situation, for the entry was going up, year after year.

In recent years rally cars had already appeared with massively over-sized tyres, the better to defeat the snow, and had been treated to axle ratio changes, to the fitments of small wheels, and to the bolting on of supercharger kits, all before the finish, and the all-important tie-deciding driving test. There was more of this to come; rallying was acutely in need of a tighter set of rules, but for the moment the most bizarre creations were acceptable.

For 1935 there were few changes to the arduous route in to Monte Carlo, but there was a complete change to the marking system. Instead of the cars completing the highest mileage always winning the event, the 'distance' bonus was eliminated, and the whole rally would swing on the results of two tests – one of them the complex 'wiggle-woggle' driving test which had been an after-event extravaganza in 1934

– which were held in Monte Carlo itself. The RAC, incidentally, tried to help British competitors by laying out a facsimile of the wiggle-woggle test at Brooklands, so that they could practise.

Every Continental starting point was allocated 1,000 points, but for no obvious reason the John O'Groats start was only allocated 987 points. Since the formula allocated to the driving tests (complicated – as every Monte Carlo rally formula ever was!) was not likely to separate the good from the mediocre by more than this, it meant that the organisers were effectively freezing out the British amateurs. The results proved it – for the highest-placed John O'Groats driver finished 50th overall.

Surprisingly enough, the result was not a massive swing away from the previously popular starting points. Although 35 crews elected to start from sunny Palermo, in Sicily (including retired racing driver Felice Nazzaro in a Fiat), there was a good line-up at Tallinn (but no likely winners), at Umea (Trevoux, Donald Healey, Humfrey Symons, 'Sammy' Davis, Jack Ridley, Lord de Clifford and a youthful Greta Molander), and at Stavanger (Stanley Barnes, C. Lahaye in his Renault, J. W. Whalley, race driver J. P. Wimille and Mme. Schell).

Among the 24 crews who had nominated John

Arrival in Monte Carlo in 1935 – the Ford V8 Model 40 of J. W. Whalley, who had driven down from Stavanger in Norway, to finish fifth overall and set second best performance by a British driver.

Pall Mall check-in at the RAC Club, on the run through to Folkestone from John O'Groats in 1935, for E. A. Denny's Riley. In a 'good-weather' year there would be time for a meal and even for a bath!

O'Groats there were several lady drivers, including Tommy Wisdom's wife 'Bill' (also in a Chrysler Airflow), Jackie Astbury, Margaret Patten, Miss M. Anderson and Fay Taylour.

As ever, it is easier to write about this winter marathon, which featured four days and four nights, more or less continuously on the road, than it was to complete it, and there is no doubt that many crews were quite exhausted when they reached the Principality.

As had happened so often in previous years, the four-strong Athens contingent was obliterated by snow (Rupert Riley actually losing his car, over a precipice, after he had managed to scramble to safety), though most other columns had an easier time – if, that is, passage over sheet ice, and through thick fog for many miles, qualifies as 'easy'.

The most sensational incident, however, involved Donald Healey. Giving the supercharged eight-cylinder Triumph Dolomite its maiden out-

ing, Healey was threading his way carefully through the fog of Denmark when his car was hit by a train as it crossed an unmarked level crossing. J. W. Whalley (who eventually finished fifth) had just preceded him.

At Monte Carlo, all cars were weighed and measured before being stowed into a *Parc Fermé*, and the crews went off to bed. The following day there were two tests. In the first the driver had to run to his car, start it up, and cross a line 30 metres away, to gain bonus marks. The amount of bonus depended on the time taken, between 30 seconds and two minutes.

Next the cars had to tackle a very complex high-speed wiggle-woggle – more officially known as an 'acceleration, braking and steering test'. Favourites like Jean Trevoux, in an Alfa Romeo Monza, were eliminated by crashes, some (like 'Sammy' Davis) finding their cars had better acceleration than brakes, and some simply got the test wrong.

Lahaye, in his Renault, was outstanding, and dry-skidded round the pylons, while Jack Ridley's showing in the tiny Triumph was also excellent. The result of the event, therefore, reflected driving test ability, and almost everyone was happy.

1935

Starting points from Amsterdam, Athens, Berlin, Bucharest, Harrogate, John O'Groats, Konigsberg, Le Mans, Lisbon, Palermo, Stavanger, Tallinn, Umea, Valencia; common route from Avignon.

	Lahaye – R. Quatresous	(Renault) Stavanger
2.	J. C. Ridley	(Triumph Gloria)
3.	Mme. L. Schell – L. Schell	(Delahaye)
4.	R. Guyot	(Renault)
5.	J. W. Whalley	(Ford V8)
6.	V. Linders	(Ford V8)

165 entries, 149 starters, 102 finishers

Victory to a Ford 'Special'

Although entries were well down on the high point of 1935, those who *did* turn up for the 1936 event were better prepared, with more special cars than ever before. The event, in any case, was also becoming very important as a publicity exercise – both for cars and a handful of famous drivers – so there was a lot of interest at the starting points, and at controls along the way.

Once again the organisers had toughened up the time schedule. Although the major part of the route was still set at a rather relaxed 40k.p.h./25m.p.h., for the last 1,000km/610 miles which approached Monte Carlo itself the target had been raised to no less than 55 k.p.h./34 m.p.h. for smaller-engined cars, and 60 k.p.h./37 m.p.h. for larger-engined cars. Even with the very best in winter-driving equipment, this was not going to be an easy trip.

Three starting points – Tallinn, Athens and John O'Groats – welcomed the majority of competitors, for old favourites like Umea (nine entrants) and Stavanger (eight entrants) had fallen well back in popularity. As in 1935, there was no commanding bonus to be gained by choosing the starting point furthest from Monte Carlo; this made everything much less predictable than in the early 1930s. Once again the wiggle-woggle test would settle the event,

but on this occasion competitors were allowed two attempts, their best time being taken in calculating the results. The results proved the point, for competitors from six starting points figured in the top 15.

Because there were still no homologation regulations to restrict a competitor's ingenuity, some of the cars were very special indeed. Christea's Ford V8 (starting from Athens) had a two-seater body style with cutaway doors, and brakes specially connected to the steering so that wheels could be locked up in the all-important driving test. Berlescu's Ford V8 was even more extraordinary, for it had an aeroplane-like style, optional skis to be applied to the front wheels in blizzard conditions, and twin rear axles!

Lahaye had a small Renault whose body hid a large engine. Donald Healey entered one of the eight-cylinder Triumph Dolomites, this time as a 2.4 litre car without a supercharger. Some of the famous names from the early 1930s – Monsieur and Madame Schell, Jean Trevoux and Dr. van Eijk amongst them – were present, along with racing drivers like Chinetti and the Hon. Brian Lewis, plus personalities like Tommy Wisdom, Humfrey Symons, and A. P. Good (driving a Lagonda from the company he had just bought).

There were 'new' names which would become more important in future years – Maurice Gatsonides, starting from Amsterdam in a Hillman Minx, David Murray (Frazer Nash) and G. Bakker Schut in a Ford V8.

The weather was more demanding than usual, though some crews, from certain starting points, had it easier than expected. The Athens route, for example, was surprisingly 'easy', and no fewer than 12 cars came through unpenalised, along with four from Bucharest.

Those electing to start from John O'Groats, on the other hand, despaired even of getting to the start and had to dig their way through; the run south was the most arduous ever experienced from this point, though the roads improved dramatically once the cars reached England again. Only 11 crews caught the scheduled boat which awaited them at Folkestone, Brian Lewis being particularly delayed.

It had not been easy for anyone, for the last run down the Rhône valley from Lyons, and across the hills from Avignon to Monte Carlo, were demanding, traffic strewn – and tackled when all crews were near the limits of their endurance. It must have been a real pleasure for them to go to bed before having to tackle the wiggle-woggle test.

In 1 min. 5 secs. of this long test P. G. Cristea (who had started from Athens) won the rally (and the £650 first prize), but not without drama. Although he had reputedly practised the test more than a hundred times in his native Rumania, he was so tensed up before the runs began that he actually took a wrong route at his first attempt. On the second run there was no mistake. Berlescu's weird-looking car actually clocked 1 min. 3.6 sec., but did not quite carry out a reversing manoeuvre correctly and was penalised.

Cristea, then, won by a margin of 0.4 seconds from the Schell's Delahaye, with Lahaye's Renault a further 1.8 seconds off the pace. Jean Trevoux's lightweight Hotchkiss was a surprising 6.7 seconds slower than Cristea, taking seventh place, while Donald Healey's Triumph (which had hydraulic brakes) had no trick methods of rounding pylons, and finished eighth.

Symons's big 25 h.p. Wolseley won the Concours, which made big headlines in the UK.

1936

Starting points from Amsterdam, Athens, Berlin, Bucharest, Glasgow, John O'Groats, Naples, Palermo, Stavanger, Tallinn, Umea, Valencia; common route from Avignon.

1. *P. G. Christea – I. Zamfirescu*   *(Ford V8) Athens*
2. *Mme. L. Schell – L. Schell*   *(Delahaye)*
3. *C. Lahaye – R. Quatresous*   *(Renault)*
4. *G. Bakker-Schut – H. de Beaufort*   *(Ford V8)*
5. *R. Guyot*   *(Renault)*
6. *R. Carriere*   *(Matford)*

105 entries, 92 starters, 72 finishers

Delahaye's racing cars dominate

Although the 1936 event had many headlines, it had not been popular with everyone, so the organisers planned big changes for 1937. Most important was the fact that the controversial wiggle-woggle test (brought into disrepute in 1936 by cars with specially modified chassis to take advantage) had been ditched in favour of a new and simpler test, and that there was to be a new 100 km. strict regularity section on the final run in to Monte Carlo. There was still no restriction on the cars, which explains how Schell's and Lebegue's Delahayes were ex-French (sports car) GP models, and how Cristea's Ford had twin rear wheels.

The unpredictable effect of all this was that entries were slow to arrive, at first, but 'on the day' more cars started than had taken the flag in 1936. Once again, however, there was a change in starting point popularity, with no fewer than 28 crews nominating Palermo, while 19 chose Umea in northern Sweden, 31 chose Stavanger in Norway, 15 chose Amsterdam, and a faithful 17 decided to start from John O'Groats. Cristea, Zamfirescu, race-driver Luigi Villoresi, Dr. van Eijk and Donald Healey all chose to start from Palermo, expecting the weather to be good – in fact there were mountainous snow drifts in northern Yugoslavia. Two of the

Amsterdam starters were actually coaches – Van der Weerd's Bedford, with 17 passengers, and Beur's Mercedes-Benz with 26 on board!

Following a leisurely (depending on weather conditions) run-in from far-flung points, the target average speeds were abruptly raised to 50 k.p.h. at Strasbourg, Paris or Bordeaux (depending on the routes chosen) for the rest of the road section. Then, for the final 100 kilometres, competitors were asked to run at a dead accurate average, their achievement to be measured by secret time checks along the route.

Every year the European weather sprang a new set of surprises. In 1937 the North Sea was so rough that ferries to Scandinavia were much delayed, this hindering the pre-rally preparations of British crews. The Athens route, having been benevolent in recent years, turned nasty once again, but on the other hand conditions in northern Europe were wintry but at least predictable. None of the Athens starters penetrated beyond Salonika. Only 63 of the 81 crews which reached Monte Carlo were unpenalised.

From Avignon to Le Muy (which measured 180 kilometres) all crews had to average between 50 and 60 k.p.h., but for the final 100 km., strict regularity at 50 k.p.h. was demanded. By comparison with later

One of the hazards of reaching Monte Carlo from the UK, in the 1930s, was the cross-Channel trip. All cars had to be hoisted on board ship, and, although it looked precarious, none seemed to be dropped, or damaged.

years this was not a demanding route, for Le Muy is a few kilometres west of Frejus, on the RN7, and the most mountainous section of the 100 km. was the run to Cannes, but there were many potential hold-ups (such as the centre of Cannes itself, and Nice for example) to be borne . . . In fact it was a lady driver, Madame Roualt (in a Matford) who set the most accurate times on this section.

After the crews had rested overnight, their cars first had to be started up (and there were penalties if this could not be done), then all had to tackle a simple driving test on the Quai Albert 1e. After a straight 200 metre sprint from rest, the car sprinted forward for the remaining 100 metres of the test. It was the sort of challenge encountered by British crews in many events during their motor sporting year.

The driving test settled everything, and on this occasion it was the fastest cars of all which shone.

Lebegue and Laurie Schell, of course, had modified sports-racing Delahayes, so it was no surprise that Schell set fastest time in 23.4 sec., though Cristea's Ford ran him close, just 0.2 sec. behind. Unhappily Schell's car had lost time on the difficult run from Stavanger, while Cristea's Ford had been penalised for bodywork infringements – his twin rear wheels projected outside the mud-guards. De Massa's Talbot, which took second place, recorded 24.0 sec., not surprising as a standard-looking body hid racing engine, gearbox and axle assemblies.

If there was unhappiness over the way that ultra-special cars won this event, there was a great deal of pleasure in seeing 'Sammy' Davis's 'works' Wolseley 25 h.p. winning the Concours competition. The European manufacturers, it was said, had quite given up hope of ever defeating the British at this specialised form of car beauty contests.

1937

Starting points from Amsterdam, Athens, Bucharest, Doncaster, John O'Groats, Konigsberg, Palermo, Stavanger, Tallinn, Umea, Vienna, Warsaw; common route from Avignon.

1.	R. Lebegue – J. Quinlin	(Delahaye 3½ litre)	Stavanger
2.	P. de Massa – N. Mahe	(Talbot)	
3.	M. Jacobs – T. de Boer	(Buick)	
4.	I. Zamfirescu – J. Trevoux	(Hotchkiss)	
5.	L. Schell – R. Dreyfus	(Delahaye)	
6.	C. Lahaye – R. Quatresous	(Renault)	

131 entries, 121 starters, 81 finishers

The first 'Col des Leques' rally

Once again the organisers re-shuffled their event, making it more of a genuine challenge. On the one hand they banned the controversial 'specials', and on the other hand they re-introduced mountain motoring into the event.

On this occasion the cars had to be based on normal production chassis, with standard saloon, or drop head coupé coachwork. Superchargers and all freak chassis fittings were banned, and at least 30 cars of one type needed to have been made by 1 November of the previous year. As to the route, all the cars were sent in from the Rhône Valley to Digne, and a special regularity section over the Col des Leques (which is on the RN85 just north west of Castellane) was planned. There would also be driving tests in Monte Carlo itself, but the straight-forward acceleration and braking test (which had favoured the 'racing cars' of 1937) had been dropped.

Once again the 'fashion' for popular starting points changed, as distance was an important factor in the marking. Of the 143 entries (which was not quite a record, but an improvement on the entry of 1936 and 1937), no fewer than 32 decided to go from Palermo, in Sicily, while an astonishing 45 chose Athens. Stavanger was still popular, as was John O'Groats, where 25 crews, all of them British, started their event.

The 1937 winner, R. Lebeque, was allocated No. One, and started from Athens, while his 1937 co-driver decided to drive his own car (a Matford) and started from Palermo. Jean Trevoux (Hotchkiss) chose Athens, Lahaye (Renault) opted for Athens – but there was no entry from Messrs. Christea or Zamfirescu, whose exploits had made headlines in recent years.

Other names which we would come to know better, in later years, were von Hanstein (from Palermo), Amadee Gordini (in a Simca, from Palermo) and Norman Garrad (in a Talbot, from John O'Groats). Many names appeared twice in the lists for, as in previous years, every driver was allowed to nominate more than one starting point, so that he could juggle with weather possibilities at the last moment.

Regular competitors left their chosen starting points in good spirits, but knew that they would be driving into the unknown from Lyons, where a 'Winter Route des Alpes' would be included in the event for the first time. Starting from Grenoble before dawn on the Saturday, not only would they have to cope with ice, snow and a tight schedule requiring average speeds of between 50 k.p.h./31 m.p.h. and 60 k.p.h./37 m.p.h., but for the first time they would also have to cope with unfamiliar roads, and a variety of twisty cols into the bargain. Not merely keeping up to schedule, but keeping going at all, might become a problem.

Although the runs in to the common meeting point at Lyons were less demanding than expected, the Winter Route was decisive. Twenty five crews were penalised on the first long section to Barreme, 24 on the second to Grasse (which included the ascent and descent of the Col des Leques, a road to become a fixture in rally mythology), and a further 13 on the third section. In some cases (such as the Col de la Croix Haute), there was thick snow at height, it was raining on to old ice at Barreme, and the descent into Castellane was very icy indeed. All in all, a real challenge which the rally had needed for some years.

Finally, after the cars and crews had had their first proper sleep for ages, there was the driving test to sort out a result, once again completely different from previous years. In a series of violent acceleration and braking maneouvres the cars had to be reversed three times, and had to make two attempts, one from each end of the sweeping Quai Albert 1e.

The story of the rally concerned René Lebegue's elegant Talbot-Darracq, for the 1937 winner was much fancied to win again. Although fastest of all throughout the first maneouvre, he failed to reverse correctly at one point on his second run, and was heavily penalised. Paul's Delahaye was also very fast, but it was the Dutch-Javanese enthusiast, Bakker Schut, who drove his low-geared Ford V8 to the absolute limit, and pipped Jean Trevoux's much more specialised Hotchkiss by tenths of second, to win the rally.

1938

Starting points from Amsterdam, Athens, Bucharest, John O'Groats, Palermo, Stavanger, Tallinn, Umea: common route from Lyons.

1. G. Bakker Schut – K. Ton   (Ford V8) Athens
2. J. Trevoux – M. Lesurque   (Hotchkiss)
3. C. Lahaye – R. Quatresous   (Renault)
4. E. Mutsaerts –
    A. Kouwemberg   (Ford V8)
5. J. Quinlin – R. Mazaud   (Matford)
6. R. A. Carriere – J. Doclos   (Matford)

143 entries, 125 starters, 94 finishers

A tie for first place!

No-one expected the 1939 rally to be exactly like that of 1938 – the Monte Carlo rally organisers were notorious for changing their views on what was a 'perfect' event – so everyone accepted the change to the format of the driving test and the inclusion of yet another special test, a speed hill climb as added interest to this winter classic.

The general format of the event, as re-jigged for 1938, had been a great success, for most crews seemed to like the idea of a *real* driving challenge through the French Alps, on the way to the Principality. This, along with long road sections from starting points all round Europe, was retained for the second year.

In one respect, however, the organisers kept their links with the past, by allocating slightly fewer bonus points to some starting points, than to others. In 1939, as in previous years, it paid to start from Athens, which was allocated 500 points, for a successful run from Bucharest or Tallinn was worth only 498 points, Stavanger or Palermo was worth only 497, while John O'Groats or Umea were worth only 496.

The four point gap between John O'Groats and Athens was enough to rule it out as a 'serious' starting point, for all the truly dedicated competitors chose Athens instead. Forty-two cars nominated Athens, including favourites like Jean Trevoux and Jean Paul, J. Quinlin, Charles Lahaye, and Dr. van Eijk, along with Tommy Wisdom, Norman Garrad, Stanley Barnes, Jack Harrap (SS-Jaguar) and many others. Twenty-four crews chose John O'Groats, including the famous *aviatrix* Amy Johnson, a young Rootes dealer called Mike Couper, and *Autocar's* 'Sammy' Davis. Even so, the Winter Route des Alpes, which effectively started from Grenoble and was split into five sections, was going to be a decisive factor, with a target average speed of 50 k.p.h./31 m.p.h.

From Grenoble, the route led over the Col de la Croix Haute to St. Julien en Bouchene, where the relatively easy second section took over. Section three, a short 12 km. dash from Barreme over the Col des Leques to Castellane, was the 'killer', and this was immediately followed by Castellane to Grasse, over the Col de Luens, before the final run through Nice led the cars into Monte Carlo itself.

Landslides near Salonika were cleared in time for Athens starters to filter through, while the Scandinavian routes encountered severe snow, but even though the average speed was jacked up in the final stages, cars in general were now so reliable, and their drivers so resourceful, that almost all fought their way through to Lyons, Grenoble, and the start of the special tests.

Conditions on the Grenoble – Monte Carlo section were far better than the organisers had hoped, the result being that most competitors managed to get close to the minimum set speeds. Over the Col des Leques, in fact, the road was entirely clear – the best that any local could remember for the past two decades. Keeping the minimum speed was no problem, so most interest was caused by observing the fastest times. Best was set by Madame Simon's Hotchkiss (12 min. 46 sec.), with six other cars (including Trevoux's Hotchkiss and Paul's Delahaye) under 13 min.

Because the Winter Route had not sorted out the field, everything hinged on results in the driving test, and in the so-called 'secret' hill climb which followed it. The driving test had reverted to its 1937 format – a 200 metre sprint, a snap reverse over a line, then a further 100 metre sprint to the finish. In 1937 it had favoured racing sports cars, and in 1939 it obviously favoured the most powerful machinery.

When all the tyre-shredding work had been done, the organisers were still in despair, for Messrs. Trevoux and Paul had set exactly the same time – 25.8 sec. – and were tied for the lead. The 1938 winner, Bakker Schut, once again in a Ford V8, had beaten them both, but as he had chosen to start from Tallinn, where there were fewer bonus points, he was immediately handicapped out of the lead.

Then came the 'secret' hill climb test, which turned out to be a twisty 1 km. climb at Eze, just off the Moyenne Corniche on the way towards Nice. Some cars had certainly practiced this, along with other possible climbs – but once again the organisers were shattered to discover that Trevoux and Paul set exactly the same times of 72.6 sec. – which were also much the fastest of the entire entry.

Trevoux and Paul had both started from Athens – carrying numbers seven and 31 – had both been unpenalised between Grenoble and Monte Carlo, had shared a time in the driving test, and were equal fastest up the Eze climb. Both had comprehensively outpaced the rest of the field.

It was the first and only time the Monte Carlo rally finished in a tie, and it was a worthy way to wind up the 1930s.

1939

Starting points from Amsterdam, Athens, Bucharest, John O'Groats, Palermo, Stavanger, Tallinn, Umea: common route from Lyons.

1.	J. Trevoux – M. Lesurque	(Hotchkiss) Athens
	J. Paul – M. Contet	(Delahaye 3½ litre) Athens
3.	E. Mutsearts – A. Kouwenberg	(Ford V8)
4.	V. Joullie-Duclos – P. Levegh	(Matford)
5.	G. Bakker Schut – P. Nortier	(Ford V8)
6.	B. Van der Hoek – K. Ton	(Ford V8)

129 entries, 121 starters, 100 finishers

1940-1948

The Second World War broke out in September 1939, and did not end until the summer of 1945. In the aftermath, it took years for Europe to re-adjust itself to peacetime again. All over mainland Europe, most especially in France, Germany, Italy and the Benelux countries, bridges were down, and the roads were in a terrible mess. Strict petrol rationing lingered – especially in the UK. Car makers took ages to get war-time *materiel* out of their systems, in order to build private cars once again.

For some time the Monte Carlo rally organisers made brave noises. In September 1946, Anthony Noghes talked about the event being held in an entirely new form in February 1947, but nothing became of this.

Motor's Sports Editor, Rodney Walkerley, was so upset by this that he decided to mount his own personal rally. Using a new Jaguar 3½ litre saloon borrowed from the factory, and accompanied by Mike Couper, he crossed the channel to Calais on 27 January and set out on a 'traditional' run via Le Mans, Bordeaux, Le Puy and Grenoble. The intrepid Brits eventually reached Monte Carlo 2 hr. 15 min. behind their self-imposed schedule, to be welcomed and feted by the organisers.

By April 1947 *Autocar*'s 'Sammy' Davis was writing that: 'Far away in the distance we can see the shadow of the Monte Carlo rally gradually becoming reality. For a Monte Carlo Rally there will be in 1948. With luck, some of the old starting places can be used . . .'. Regulations were actually published in October, with six starting points projected, but in December it was called off again, for the French government would not authorise petrol for the event.

In 1949, however, there was no hiccup. Ten years after the last pre-war event, the Monte Carlo road show was on the road again!

Part 2:
Timekeeping before performance, concours before function

1949

Revival after a ten-year gap

When the regulations for the 1949 event arrived, they were seen to be those of 1948, with only the dates altered. There were, however, considerable changes compared with the last Monte which had been run, ten years earlier in 1939.

Anthony Noghes and his co-organisers had to take note of post-war austerity, a shortage of fuel in some areas, and poor road conditions where war-time damage had not totally been repaired.

On this occasion the route was based on a long circuit of Western Europe, from Monte Carlo to Monte Carlo, via Strasbourg, Amsterdam, Paris and Lyon. The route from six other start points joined the main circuit at various controls, and all had to complete about 2,000 miles before reaching Monte Carlo.

For the first time since the 1920s, there was no starting point from John O'Groats. Instead the British contigent began their journey from Glasgow at 17.21 hr. on 24 January; there was an intermediate control at Doncaster before cars made the familiar Folkestone-Boulogne cross-channel journey. The circuit was joined at Luxembourg, the cars then having to go north to Amsterdam before making determined tracks towards the Mediterranean sun.

Compared with 1939 the average speed schedule

had risen sharply, for cars had to average 50 k.p.h-/31 m.p.h. throughout. If the weather had been as bad as feared this might have caused wholesale chaos, but as it happened there were few problems with snow and ice. In 1949, as in 1939, the only aid to traction was by strap-on chains.

It was such a relief to get back to peace-time conditions that the 1949 entry hit an all-time record. No fewer than 205 cars started – 47 of them from Glasgow – this being the start of the post-war Monte 'band-waggon effect' which would peak in 1953, when more than 400 cars set out for Monte Carlo.

The weather was much kinder than usual, even for the crews starting from Oslo and Stockholm, the result being that most crews made it to Monte Carlo without penalty, many having had time for leisurely meals, even baths, at major time controls. The result, therefore, would all hinge on a car's performance in the special tests.

On this occasion, there were no special tests on the way through the Alpes Maritimes to the Principality – the organisers had hoped the weather would thin out the runners for them. Instead, and after a night's rest in Monte Carlo, all crews had to tackle a speed and regularity test in the mountains behind the town; although the route was supposed to be secret every taxi driver seemed to know of it, and that it included the Mont des Mules, so many a recce was made in advance...

Although the total distance of this test was only 17.5 km. it was a demanding exercise. Each crew had to complete the loop three times – the first, effectively, for an official 'practice' session. Two 3 km. sectors had to be completed as fast as possible *and* in exactly the same time, with a longer (10 km.) sector to be completed at an average speed of at least 50 k.p.h.

Clearly the fastest cars and the bravest drivers (plus, let it be admitted, those who had managed to practise...) had the advantage. At the end of the event, therefore, it was no surprise to see Jean Trevoux's Hotchkiss victorious once again (his car was said to have a 110 m.p.h. top speed), and to see seasoned British drivers like Leslie Potter (Allard) and Ken Wharton ('works' Ford Pilot) well in contention.

For the British there was also the pleasure in seeing St. Albans motor trader Mike Couper winning the Concours de Confort in his Bentley Mk VI; he also finished 25th in the rally itself, no mean achievement for such a large car.

This was the year in which the BBC decided that the rally was good news copy (albeit of the 'nudge-nudge, isn't this crazy' variety). Because most manufacturers were still struggling to establish their post-war models, few had had time to enter 'works' teams. However, with public and media interest so obviously rising fast, they would not make that mistake again.

1949

Starting points from Florence, Glasgow, Lisbon, Monte Carlo, Oslo, Prague, Stockholm: common route from Rheims.

1. J. Trevoux – M. Lesurque (Hotchkiss) Lisbon
2. M. Worms – E. Mouche (Hotchkiss)
3. F. Dobry – Z. Treybal (Bristol 400)
4. L. Potter – R. Richards (Allard)
5. K. Wharton – J. Gibson (Ford Pilot)
6. J. Laroche – R. Radix (Salmson)

225 entries, 205 starters, 166 finishers

Only five clean sheets on the road

For 1950, British entries leapt to a new height, with 75 from the total of 308. Once again the British starting point was Glasgow (with 70 cars listed), but again the most popular starting point was Monte Carlo itself, with 104 on the list.

Even though the organisation of the 1949 event had threatened to come apart at the seams from time to time (most people put this down to the new officials' inexperience), this had mostly been concerned with the working out of the special test results. The main route was as before – a long circuit from Monte Carlo to Monte Carlo, with other routes joining in along the way: Glasgow starters, therefore, paused briefly at Doncaster, crossed the Channel from Folkestone, and joined up at Luxembourg. Cars began leaving Glasgow at 15.11 hrs. and were due at Folkestone at 07.36 hrs. the following day. In 1950, however, there was no major hold-up at Boulogne for an enforced party.... In 1949 the speed and regularity test had not been popular with anyone (it was said that officials refused to struggle through *that* sort of calculation marathon again – there were no computers in 1950!), but it was repeated for 1950. Also, having arrived in the Principality all crews were obliged to complete an acceleration/braking test.

The most numerous British cars were Allards and Jowett Javelins, but this year also saw the first appearance of a 'works' Rootes team of Sunbeam-Talbot 90s, driven by Norman Garrad, George Hartwell and John Pearman.

Compared with 1949, the weather was awful – which, as far as the organisers were concerned, meant that it was perfect. South of Paris, on the run down to the Mediterranean, a blizzard set in soon after the first cars (the Lisbon starters) had passed through. The Glasgow contingent had a truly horrid time, yet the expert crews still struggled through. The traditional route across the mountains from Lyons, via Grasse, was icy, deep in snow, or both at the same time. Even twice-winner Jean Trevoux (driving a Delahaye instead of his more familiar Hotchkiss) was delayed behind a snow-plough and lost his clean sheet at Grasse. More than half the rally was eliminated by the weather.

Here was a Monte well and truly to be won 'on the road', for only those cars with clean sheets would be allowed to take part in the speed/regularity test. Hard luck stories were everywhere. Sydney Allard (driving one of his own cars) was fastest in the acceleration/braking test, but had lost a mere three minutes on the road sections – he could only finish eighth. Racing driver Louis Rosier (Renault 4CV) had been first on the road before Grasse, but went off the road near that town, and could not retrieve his car. A future Monte 'legend', Peter Harper, made his Monte début in a Hillman Minx, started from Glasgow and finished as a very creditable 15th overall.

As so often in the past, the choice of starting point had been critical. Those at the front of the cavalcade (especially those starting from Monte Carlo and Lisbon) had the best of the weather – no fewer than 24 of the first 50 started from Monte Carlo. There were 10 from Lisbon, and eight each from Glasgow and Stockholm. No-one else got a look-in.

Only five crews lost no time at all – one from Lisbon, the other four from Monte Carlo, a Hotchkiss, a Humber, and three Simcas, these being the only cars allowed to take part in the speed/regularity test on the Mont des Mules.

Somehow everyone had expected a Hotchkiss to be at the top, though the surprise was that it was Maurice Becquart rather than Jean Trevoux who was driving the car. The rival Simca 8s were well-known as compact Fiat-designed sports saloons and coupés. At the end of the test Becquart's Hotchkiss had put up best performance – which made it six Hotchkiss victories, in two straight hat-tricks – with the major surprise being Maurice Gatsonides's amazing performance in the vast 4.1 litre Humber Snipe, one of the largest *and* heaviest cars in the event. 'Gatso' finished second, penalised a mere 1.38 seconds more than the winning car – even so his finest Monte performance was still three years into the future.

Once again Mike Couper won the Grand Prix in the Concours de Confort, this time in a Park Ward-bodied Rolls-Royce Silver Wraith. So what, you might say? The fact is that the car was seriously crashed in the blizzard, needed a new front wing to be hand-beaten in 16 hours at the Rolls-Royce dealership in Monte Carlo, and it won the event with one headlamp missing!

1950

Starting points from Florence, Glasgow, Lisbon, Monte Carlo, Oslo, Stockholm: common route from Rheims

1. *M. Becquart – M. Secret* (Hotchkiss) Lisbon
2. *M. Gatsonides –*
   K. S. Barendregt (Humber Super Snipe)
3. *Quinlin – J. Behra* (Simca 8)
4. *Scaron – Pascal* (Simca 8)
5. *Dr. Angelvin – Chaboud* (Simca 8)
6. *I. Wollert* (Buick)

308 entries, 282 starters, 136 finishers

Trevoux's fourth victory

Once again the entry list expanded, and the organisers accepted no fewer than 362 cars, 70 of which had British crews. Applications for entries had to be channelled through the RAC; there was so much 'Monte fever' at this time, however, that the 70 crews had to be chosen from 600 applicants.

There was one real bombshell in the regulations – that a car would only be eligible if its engine was manufactured by the maker of the chassis! At a stroke this eliminated cars like the Allards and Healeys. At first it was even thought likely to eliminate other marques such as Triumph (whose engines were made by Standard), MG (engines made by Morris) and Bentley (engines by Rolls-Royce) but such anomalies were soon ironed out.

Compared with 1950, there were several important route changes. The basic Monte Carlo – Monte Carlo 'merry-go-round' route, with other routes joining in, was retained. However, British crews starting from Glasgow were obliged to reach Folkestone via a control at Llandrindod Wells, and the main route was joined at Liège (instead of Luxembourg as in the previous two years).

Instead of starting from Florence, Italian crews began their trip from Palermo in Sicily, and joined in the loop as late as Bourges; not surprisingly only 12

chose to do this, and seven of them had dropped out by the time the event reached Rome! The 'hot' money for an easy trip was on Lisbon (Trevoux and Becquart had both won from there in 1949 and 1950) – the most popular starting points being Monte Carlo, Lisbon, Stockholm and Glasgow.

From Britain 'works' interest was growing, with strong teams entered by Ford, Jowett and Sunbeam-Talbot. Such teams were now used to practising difficult sections of the route in advance. The RAC even gave British crews a chance to practise the compulsory speed and maneouvring test held on the Promenade after arrival, by laying out a replica of the test at Silverstone. The unpopular Mont des Mules 'speed and regularity' test in the mountains – so unpopular in 1949 and 1950 – had been abandoned, and had been replaced by a similar trial on the Monaco Grand Prix circuit, which would be tackled by the top 50.

Before the rally began, forecasts were that the tough motoring would begin in the Massif Central, with the Clermont Ferrand-Le Puy-Valance section expected to be critical. In the event the weather was much kinder than expected, but only 108 of the 337 starters reached Monte Carlo without losing time on the road. There was much snow in the Alpes around

Castellane and Grasse, but everyone seemed well prepared for this.

Then came the test on arrival, where 'Montemaster' Jean Trevoux set fastest time (22.6 sec.) in his very sleek-looking 108 b.h.p., 4½ litre Delahaye. Cecile Vard's Jaguar Mk V recorded 23.1 sec., and the Comte de Monte Real, 23.2 sec. in a big vee-8-engined Ford. Ken Wharton's Ford Pilot was close behind, as were the 'works' Jowett Jupiters of R. F. Ellison and Gordon Wilkins.

After a night's rest, 50 drivers tackled a 'Round the Houses' test on the famous Monaco GP circuit. Cars started in batches of three, were allowed two practice circuits, and four laps in the actual test. Both speed and regularity were required and co-drivers could not be carried; marking was complex, but most drivers went for speed rather than safety. Louis Chiron, in the other special-coachwork Delahaye set several laps at 51 m.p.h., but complete and utter consistency was achieved by Peter Bolton's Bristol and W. H. Waring's Jaguar Mk V.

Even though Trevoux was not as regular as had been expected, his earlier test time had been outstanding. In the end, he won from Comte de Monte Real by 26.76 marks to 27.12, while Northern Ireland's Cecil Vard finished third, at 27.43. It was another good year for the British, with Ellison's Jowett and Wharton's Ford tying for sixth place, Waring ninth and Wilkins 10th. Jowett won their capacity class *and* one of the team prizes.

Naturally, Mike Couper's Bentley Mk VI won the Concours de Confort, this time with a car featuring rotary wipers on the headlamps.

Statisticians had a heyday. Not only was this Trevoux's fourth outright victory – his others having been in 1934, 1939 and 1949 – but it was the third consecutive occasion on which the winning car had started from Lisbon. Was a post-War pattern setting in?

1951

Starting points from Glasgow, Lisbon, Monte Carlo, Oslo, Palermo, Stockholm: common route from Bourges

1.	*J. Trevoux – R. Crovetto*	*(Delahaye) Lisbon*
2.	*Comte de Monte Real –*	
	M. J. Palma	*(Ford V8)*
3.	*C. Vard – A. Young*	*(Jaguar Mk V)*
4.	*G. Gautruche – R. Giriez*	*(Citroën Six)*
5.	*L. Chiron – N. Mahé*	*(Delahaye)*
6.=	*R. F. Ellison*	
	– W. H. Robinson	*(Jowett Jupiter)*
	K. Wharton – J. Langelaan	*(Ford Pilot)*

362 entries, 337 starters, 283 finishers

Sydney Allard's famous victory

For the 1952 rally there were two big changes – one was the introduction of a demanding 74 km. regularity circuit behind the Principality and the other was that 1951's ill-considered ban on cars without 'own-make' engines was abandoned. This year's oddity, however, was that all cars had to be less than three years old...

As far as the British enthusiast was concerned, however, 1952 was a real land-mark in Monte Carlo rally history. Not only did a British driver win (for the first time since 1931), but he was using a car of his own make! Almost as newsworthy was the fact that racing driver Stirling Moss started the event in a Sunbeam-Talbot 90 – and finished second overall.

Although the rally could have accepted 420 cars, only 369 entries were taken up, 92 of which were British. Sixty-nine elected to start from Glasgow, and 14 more from Monte Carlo itself – those crews combining the journey down with a last-minute reconnaisance session, particularly of the regularity test. As before Jaguars, Jowetts, Rileys and Sunbeam-Talbots were the most popular British marques. That doyen of Fleet Street, Tommy Wisdom, was partnered by Lord Selsdon, and elected to use a vast 5½ litre Daimler Straight-Eight model. Mercedes-Benz made a return to motor sport by entering a trio

of 220s, driven by no less than the GP racing team of Karl Kling, Rudolf Caracciola and Hermann Lang!

As ever, the 'core' of the routes was the Monte Carlo-Amsterdam-Monte Carlo loop. Glasgow starters reached Folkestone via Llandrindod Wells as usual, and for everyone the rough stuff started from Bourges, south of Paris.

As in 1950, towards the end of the concentration runs the event was very difficult indeed. The statistics – as *The Autocar* commented – summarise it all. Of 328 cars starting the rally, only 167 reached the finish; of them, a mere 15 cars had lost no time on the road. Of the Glasgow starters, only Sydney Allard made it on time. Of the section after Bourges, *The Autocar*'s report stated:

'What then happened on the Bourges-Valence section would fill several books, yet leave much untold. At the best of times it is a twisty, rather dangerous, run. Now, suddenly, came snow storms, with the result that the cars ran into what seemed a barrage of whirling white flakes...'

The Col des Leques section, down towards Grasse, was little better, but at least it was daylight.

It was one of the most difficult Montes of recent

memory – recalling some of the demonic events of the 1930s when cars were not as fast or sophisticated, and when heating systems were non-existent; 1952 conditions encountered 20 years earlier, on the same roads, would have obliterated much of the event.

After a much-needed night's rest, only 50 crews were eligible to tackle the regularity test. This was a 74.4 km. loop starting and finishing from the Moyenne Corniche at the bottom of the Monte des Mules road. The route led over the Mont des Mules, the Cols de Nice, Braus, and Castillon – it being the Braus, with all its tight hairpins, which would cause the trouble. The set average speed was 45 k.p.h./27.9 m.p.h. (originally it had been set at 50 k.p.h./31 m.p.h., but the authorities had refused this on the grounds that it was dangerous). There would be public, and secret, checks by officials, but the cars would not stop at any of them; each competing car had its rally plate on the nose, and a colour wash on the front wings to give advance warning.

Even though much of the loop, and *all* the cols, were snow-covered, some crews kept immaculate time. If Stirling Moss had not inadvertently gone off the road at one point he would surely have won; if the roads had been less slippery Louis Rossier's Talbot Lago would have figured more strongly. If, if, if . . . As it was, Sydney Allard, accompanied in his own P1 saloon by Guy Warburton and Tom Lush, swept serenely round the course, lost a total of 130 sec. on absolute regularity – and beat Stirling Moss by 4 sec.! Mercedes-Benz's Grand Prix drivers won the team prize, and no other British crew finished in the first 20.

After this, Mike Couper's great achievement in winning the Concours de Confort for the fourth year in succession (once again using a Bentley Mk VI) was almost missed.

1952

Starting points from Glasgow, Lisbon, Monte Carlo, Munich, Oslo, Palermo, Stockholm: common route from Bourges.

1. S. H. Allard – G. Warburton
      – T. Lush   (Allard) Glasgow
2. S. Moss – D. Scannell
      – J. Cooper   (Sunbeam-Talbot 90)
3. Dr. Angelvin
      – Ms. Angelvin   (Simca Sport)
4. R. Cotton – L. Didier   (Jaguar Mk V)
5. M. Becquart – H. Ziegler   (Jowett Jupiter)
6. K. Heurtaux – M. Crespin   (Jaguar Mk VII)

369 entries, 328 starters, 167 finishers

1953

Gatsonides's precision wins for Ford

You could almost measure the recovery in post-War Europe by the surge of interest in the Monte Carlo. In 1949 there had been 225 entries, in 1950 308, and by 1952 no fewer than 369 had entered. But that wasn't the limit – in 1953 the organisers accepted no fewer than 440 entries; this was an all-time record that would never again be approached.

Demand from British drivers was staggering, and well over the RAC's allocation. In the end 114 were accepted, almost all of whom started from Glasgow. It was no surprise that the most popular British car in the lists was the Sunbeam-Talbot 90, of which there were 31 examples.

The money must have stretched further in those halcyon days, for eight of the Sunbeam-Talbots were works-supported, with Stirling Moss obviously being the star driver. Ford were strongly represented, with a team of Zephyr Sixes prepared at the Lincoln Cars depot on the Great West Road, across the road from the now-demolished Firestone factory.

The route was almost exactly the same as in 1952, which meant the Glasgow starters drove to Llandrindod Wells before making for Dover, while the Monte Carlo starters completed a loop via Strasbourg, Amsterdam, Paris and Le Puy in the Massif Central. If the snows held off there would be no hard driving before the cavalcade arrived at Monte Carlo – but in wintry weather the difficult motoring would begin after Clermont Ferrand.

It was, in fact, a very easy year for weather. No fewer than 253 of the 404 starters reached Monte Carlo without road penalty. Even the traditional hazard of the Col des Leques, linking Digne to Castellane was almost clear.

It was not all plain sailing, however. In his book *Rallying to Monte Carlo* the experienced Mike Couper nominated the St. Flour-Le Puy-Valance section as the most difficult. Driving an R-Type Bentley saloon as hard as possible, he was 19 min. early at Le Puy, then took the long (and easy) way round but had only 13 min. in hand at Valence. The redoubtable Maurice Gatsonides (in a 'works' Ford Zephyr) took the short and wintry route from Le Puy to Valence and made it by a mere 2 min.!

After a night's rest in Monte Carlo, every competitor had to complete the 275 yard acceleration, braking, reversing and sprinting test, after which the fastest 100 cars would be selected to compete in the same mountain regularity test as had been used in 1952. Driving test results were only used to select the hundred – but the times were never used in assessing final penalties.

Ian and Pat Appleyard finished second in 1953, turning in almost perfect regularity in their big Jaguar Mk VII. The light patch on the front wings was a colour wash applied by the organisers so that controllers could pick out the cars at secret checks. This is the descent of the infamous Col de Braus section.

The driving test favoured the fastest cars, but the 74 km./46 mile regularity loop favoured the most meticulous navigators.

In reality, therefore, the 'real rally' had started in the *Massif Central*, a full two days after competitors had left their starting points and toured towards Central France at a 31 m.p.h./50 k.p.h. average speed. Even so, the choice of cars tackling the regularity test was to be settled by a mere 20-odd sec. of fast, but straight-line, driving. Was this what world-class rallying was meant to be about?

The 1952 Monte winner, Sydney Allard (driving the latest version of his own product), set fastest time in the test, in 21.8 sec., yet only 4.1 sec. separated him from the 100th competitor. All the expected crews made it, and the scene was set for a carefully-navigated final test.

Once again crews found that the front wings of their cars had been covered with a hideous yellow colour wash (to make them easily visible to the timekeepers), and on this occasion there were to be six declared control points in the loop, but no secret checks. To deter crews from dawdling, their time over the last 200 metres before the control had to take less than 24 sec., and had to be completed non-stop. The set average speed – which was only announced as 47 k.p.h./29.2 m.p.h. when the first cars lined up for the start – was enough to make everyone hurry up and down the Cols de Castillon and Braus.

Because the weather was so mild – only a few patches of ice and snow lay around in the shadows – this was the classic rallying precision test, which many crews had already practised in advance. Various average speed computations had been made, but in the end it all came down to spirited driving, careful time-keeping, and the professional use of that miraculous instrument, the 'Mark 1 eyeball'.

Rallying's wily old character, Maurice Gatsonides, co-driven by Peter Worledge, drove his Zephyr so accurately that he lost a mere *two seconds* (one at each of two controls) in the loop, while Ian and Pat Appleyard lost three sec. (a two sec. and a one sec. error) - it was enough to give 'Gatso', and Ford of Britain, their first-ever Monte Carlo victory.

On this occasion the Grand Prix in the Concours competition was won by B. Proos Hoogendijk's Sunbeam-Talbot 90.

1953

Starting points from Glasgow, Lisbon, Monte Carlo, Munich, Oslo, Palermo, Stockholm: common route from Bourges

1. M. Gatsonides – P. Worledge   (Ford Zephyr) Monte Carlo
2. I. Appleyard
    – Ms. P. Appleyard   (Jaguar Mk VII)
3. R. Marion – J. Charmasson   (Citroën Six)
4. M. Grosgogeat – P. Biagini   (Panhard 750)
5. C. Vard – A. R. Jolley   (Jaguar Mk V)
6. S. Moss – D. Scannell
    – J. Cooper   (Sunbeam-Talbot 90)

440 entries, 404 starters, 346 finishers

Controversy over Chiron's Lancia win

After 1953 it was clear that mild weather made the existing rally format altogether too easy. Even so, the changes made for 1954 were not likely to turn the event into a real drivers' rally.

For the traditional concentration runs the well-established Monte Carlo-Amsterdam-Paris-Monte Carlo loop was retained. However, to bring back some of the challenge, an Athens starting point was re-introduced for the first time since 1939. The Balkans weather, it was thought, might still be very demanding, but the cars had improved considerably since then.

Although the total entry was slightly down on 1953, no fewer than 148 cars were of British manufacture. Thirty-two of them were Ford Zephyrs (this was an obvious reaction to Gatsonides's 1953 win), 21 were Jaguars and 19 were Sunbeam-Talbots. As usual many more British crews had tried to enter than could be accepted – nevertheless the 121 British entries was the biggest of all, with 118 French crews next up.

For the British starters there were no novelties, for the 90 starters on the Glasgow-Llandrindod Wells-Dover route was the same as in 1953. For everyone, though, there was the challenge of a much longer, and more serious, regularity test in the

mountains, while a Monaco GP circuit test was re-introduced after a two year lay-off.

The regularity test stretched from the French town of Gap to Monte Carlo, a 254 km./164 mile run split into four sections of 126, 12, 67 and 59 kilometres respectively. Competitors could choose any average speed between 45 k.p.h. and 60 k.p.h., then hold it for each section. The average recorded on the short second section (up and over the Col des Leques, north-west of Castellane) would be taken as the 'master' by the organisers.

It would not, however, have been the Monte without a complex formula to sort out a result – this actually involving the time taken over the Col des Leques and the average speed time errors over the other sections. A 10-minute study of the formula showed that this *was* a speed contest after all, and that the fastest passes of the Col des Leques *combined* with accurate average speed keeping would be critical!

Here, more than ever, was a case for reconnaissance, for the first section would be complete before the Col des Leques was tackled – and if there was more snow and ice than expected the team's efforts might be in ruins. After that, of course, the five-lap circuit test (run to a formula which penalised the

Rushing down from the mountains in the Alpes Maritimes *in 1954 come a Dutch-registered Jaguar Mk VII and a Peugeot 203. No sign of snow at this altitude, in a town not far from Nice, or Digne.*

larger-engined cars) would only serve to 'tune' the results a little, with the fastest drivers pulling up a little through the order.

Is that clear, now? Most crews thought it was, except that on arrival at the start of the previously practised Col des Leques test they found that the kilometre marker stone had actually been moved – the organisers, it was said, had 're-surveyed' the route and adjusted the position of the stone by a significant distance. This, of course, was a piece of French, not Monegasque municipal hardware...

The Autocar summarised the mild weather perfectly:

'This must surely go down in Monte Carlo Rally history as the year in which the weather did its utmost to spoil the event... Only from Athens was the going bad... On the traditional routes conditions were unbelievably good...'

Even so, only three of the Athens starters were unpenalised by the time they reached Belgrade, in Yugoslavia. In the end, just 32 of the 361 starters retired on the run down to Monte Carlo, of which a mere 67 had lost any time.

The Gap-Monte Carlo regularity test started at daybreak on Thursday, 21st January, and the race over the N85 to Nice, and then to Monte Carlo itself, began. Most of the serious 'works' competitors chose to gamble on the Col des Leques being clear, and were fast throughout – Stirling Moss averaged 63.4 k.p.h./39.4 m.p.h., Gatsonides was just a shade slower, while the eventual winner, Louis Chiron (in the brand-new 2½ litre Lancia Aurelia GT Coupé), averaged 60.0 k.p.h./37.3 m.p.h.

Not only was Chiron fast but his navigator, C. Basadonna, was very accomplished, so he was clearly in the lead at the end of the day. Even so, Pierre David's Peugeot 203 had performed remarkably well, as had several other crews in small-engined French cars. British drivers were not quite as successful as usual, but the expected names – Ronnie Adams and Cevil Vard (Jaguar Mk VIIs), 'Cuth' Harrison (Ford Zephyr) and Stirling Moss (Sun-

The line-up of finishers on the Casino terrace, in Monte Carlo in 1954. Two newly-formed British teams were present on this occasion – Daimler Conquest saloons, and Armstrong-Siddeley Sapphires. Both 'works' efforts were short-lived.

Top Photo, p. 91,
The Rootes Group's 'works' team for 1954 included an experienced ladies' crew – left to right Sheila Van Damm, Anne Hall and Françoise Clarke. Although pipped for the Coupe des Dames, they shared in the Manufacturers' Team Prize award.

Bottom photo, p. 91,
Rush-hour at the famous 'gas-works' hairpin on the Monaco GP circuit in 1954 – the cars involved include Jaguar Mk VII, Panhard, Peugeot 203, DKW Sonderklasse and Porsche 356.

Desolation, but not much sign of winter, in 1954, with the Standard Vanguard crew of J. Stoddart and W. Stoddart, who had started from Glasgow, pressing on to the finish.

beam-Talbot 90) – were all prominent.

As expected, Chiron's Lancia was outstanding on the circuit test, but there was great controversy afterwards when it was suggested that not enough of those cars had actually been built – homologation squabbles, it seems, are nothing new!

Rootes, as usual, put up a splendid team show, winning the Charles Faroux Challenge Trophy, even though one of their drivers, Leslie Johnson, suffered a suspected heart-attack on the regularity run and had to be rushed to hospital on arrival.

Starting points from Athens, Glasgow, Lisbon, Monte Carlo, Munich, Oslo, Palermo and Stockholm: common route from Valence

1. L. Chiron – C. Basadonna (*Lancia Aurelia GT*) *Monte Carlo*
2. P. David – P. Barbier (*Peugeot 203*)
3. A. Blanchard – A. Lecoq (*Panhard 750*)
4. C. Johansson – G. Jensen (*Renault 4CV*)
5. J. Vial – G. Panuel (*Renault 4CV*)
6. R. J. Adams – J. Titterington (*Jaguar Mk VII*)

402 entries, 363 starters, 329 finishers

1955

Private Sunbeam beats the 'works' team

Perhaps the 1954 event had been rather too predictable, and the regularity test too easily 'learned' by the professional crews. Perhaps it was merely that the organising team was once again ready to meddle with a popular formula. The Concentration Runs from eight far-flung cities were modified considerably, while the difficult part of the event – the speed/regularity test from Gap to Monte Carlo, was altered and made 'secret'.

From Glasgow the 105 entries were faced with a different way of reaching Dover. Starting from Glasgow (the first car at 2.05 p.m.), the route led to a control at Stranraer, on the south-west tip of Scotland, then returned to Doncaster, passed through London and reached Dover at 8.15 a.m. the next morning.

For the first time since 1949 the concept of a 'core' route from Monte Carlo to Monte Carlo via Amsterdam was abandoned, with most routes converging on the Rheims-Vesoul-Valence axis. Monte Carlo starters went via Pau, Perigueux and Rheims, while the Athens and Palermo starters joined in at Valence.

To cut down on the practising which had been rife in 1954, the organisers said that the speed/regularity test from Gap to Monte Carlo would

follow any one of six routes, and that they would not choose the route, nor specify the set average speed, until the day of the rally arrived. Since two of these routes crossed the Cols d'Allos, and de la Cayolle (both of which would certainly be closed by snow in January), the choice was in any case restricted to four routes. In the event the information was given out at the Chambery control, several hours in advance, but a great deal of mathematical calculation (sometimes carried out by the navigator while the rally was on its way south to Gap) was needed.

There was a further sting in the tail. Instead of a 10-minute race round the houses in Monaco, there was an acceleration, braking and manoeuvring test on the quayside, followed by a demanding 200-mile Mountain Circuit for the best 100 crews to sort out the best of all.

There had been so much recent British success in European rallies that new teams were springing up. The most significant new organisations were the BMC team, managed by Marcus Chambers, and the Standard-Triumph team managed by Ken Richardson. For the Monte Carlo rally not only Aston Martin, but Armstrong-Siddeley and Daimler all entered teams as well.

Once again the organisers were let down by the

weather, for the Concentration Routes, though slippery and treacherous in many places, were all passable. The result was that 319 cars started, but only 48 were forced to retire, and many crews were unpenalised on the road. Packed snow began to feature south of Grenoble but, even so, many of the 'traditional' snowy roads in the *Alpes Maritimes* had clear stretches.

The Gap-Monte Carlo regularity test was 'Option 4' of the six routes; it was 333 km./207 miles long and was divided into five sections. Set averages exceeded 60 k.p.h./37 m.p.h. in places – this, make no mistake, was something of a winter road race. The longest section, of 100 km., was a 'settling-in' run via Seyne-les-Alpes and Digne; the toughest was that old favourite, the Col des Leques, allied to the run round the side of a lake to Barrage de Castillon; this had been set at a speed faster than that achieved by Stirling Moss in 1954 and was impossible for everyone. After that the run to Monte Carlo was a relief, even though the section through Nice was set at the highest speed of all.

The fact that the organisers also imposed secret checks (timing was 'on sight', cars were not stopped nor were their cards marked, so they had no chance to argue with marshals) didn't help; even the experienced Gatsonides, in an Aston Martin DB2/4, was penalised at one of them.

After arrival in Monte Carlo and the manoeuvring test, the provisional order put Marang's six-cylinder Citroën in the lead, with Delliere's Salmson and Hopfen's DKW behind him, and the Norwegian, Per Malling (Sunbeam Mk III) in fourth place. Gerry Burgess's Ford Zephyr lay ninth, the Appleyards' Jaguar Mk VII 10th, and Ronnie Adams's Jaguar 11th.

On the Saturday, 100 crews tackled a difficult 200-mile regularity run, which was split into six long sections. This was no easy trundle around the mountains close to Monte Carlo, but a red-blooded expedition up the valley of the Var, over the Col de Valberg to Guillaumes, up and over the Col St. Martin to St. Martin Vesubie, then over the Cols du Turini, St. Jean, Braus and Castillon before returning to the Principality via Menton.

For Ian Appleyard the tragedy was that his Jaguar engine blew a core plug, and several cars crashed out on slippery, but not very snowy, going. Malling's car pulled up to win the event, Marang's Citroën slipped to 10th, while Burgess leapt to fourth, Gatsonides to seventh, with Ronnie Adams (eighth), Peter Harper (ninth) and Sheila Van Damm (11th and the *Coupés des Dames*) close behind. Jaguar won the team prize, so almost everyone was happy.

1955

Starting points from Athens, Glasgow, Lisbon, Monte Carlo, Munich, Oslo, Palermo and Stockholm: common route from Valence.

1. P. Malling – G. Fadum (Sunbeam Mk III) Oslo
2. G. Gillard – R. Duget (Panhard 850)
3. H. Gerdum – J. Kuhling (Mercedes-Benz 220)
4. G. Burgess – P. Easton (Ford Zephyr)
5. W. Schock – R. Moll (Mercedes-Benz 220)
6. W. Lier – H. Ziegler (Lancia Aurelia)

362 entries, 319 starters, 273 finishers

Jaguar (Ronnie Adams) – another British win

While the 1955 event had been a success, for 1956 the format was changed once again. Not only was the Monte Carlo start abandoned, but so was the Palermo starting point. In its place the Italian contingent (only 13 of them) started from Rome, then spent the first day driving south to the Gulf of Taranto, then looping north, up the Adriatic coast to Rimini, before making for Klagenfurt, Stuttgart, and Paris.

Little change, at least, for the Glasgow starters, who visited Stranraer and Barnby Moor (Ye Olde Bell Hotel) on their way to Dover. Once in France, however, they faced a long drive south to Aurillac, then back up to Rheims and Paris, before finally turning south towards the Mediterranean.

As the rally approached the Alps, too, there was a new look to the event. As *The Autocar* report began:

'The old order has changed for the Monte Carlo rally. New routes, new names... the Col des Leques has gone, and this year competitors are talking of the Col du Granier, the gorges of the Bourne and the Col du Rousset, three crucial parts of the special test from Paris to Monaco, lying between Chambery and St. Die, over which category the cars (normal saloons) had to average just over 33 m.p.h. and category two (*Gran Turismo* and modified saloons) just over 36 m.p.h.'

None of these novelties frightened off the entrants, who numbered 351 (compared with 362 in 1955). Seventy-three cars started from Glasgow, the first leaving at the relatively civilised time of 5.24 a.m. One entrant, Dr. Mitchell, got just 200 yards down the hill before crashing into a Glasgow Corporation bus... for the others it was an easy, if icy, run to Dover by 10 p.m.

Compared with 1955, there was less 'works' interest, though BMC, Standard-Triumph, Ford and Rootes (Sunbeam) all entered teams of cars. It was sad to see that the Appleyards had retired from rallying without winning the event, but several other Jaguar drivers were hoping to take over where they had left off. All French eyes were on the space-age Citroën DS19s, tackling their first major rally – was the combination of front-wheel-drive and self-levelling suspension going to be unbeatable?

As in 1955, there would be three 'Classification Tests' – the first covering the run from Chambery to Monte Carlo, with difficult average speed targets and secret checks to get in the way, the second a *downhill* speed and braking test on the Monte des Mules into the very outskirts of Monte Carlo, and the third being a difficult drive over most of the snow-covered cols north of the Principality, including the Turini, St. Roche, l'Orme, and Braus.

As in 1955, and in several post-War years, weather conditions were surprisingly mild. Old hands wondered when the Monte would next be blitzed by the weather – in fact they had two more years to wait, for 1958 would generate many horror stories! In the Massif Central it was raining, and the temperature was above freezing. Even Yugoslavian conditions were benign. Two-hundred-and-seventy-two cars congregated in Paris, only eight of them penalised.

South of Chambery the passage of the three cols – Granier, Cucheron and Porte – was familiar enough, even in thick fog, but the run through Villard de Lans, through a tunnel at the top of the Col du Rousset and down into Die was most certainly not. *That*, the competitors grumbled, was Alpine rally territory – and the Alpine was welcome to it. In truly wintry weather this section could have been a stopper, but in January 1956 it was merely a difficult time-keeping exercise.

Seasoned drivers like Sheila Van Damm and Sydney Allard lost time in the fog, while Leslie Brooke's Standard 10 arrived at the final La Turbie control with a collapsed rear wheel – he made it on time, just.

Most crews had time to wait, bask in the January sun, and prepare for the Mont des Mules test, a flat-out dash, with an emergency stop at the end of it, which took a mere 40-odd seconds for the brave.

In Monte Carlo, after a night's sleep, the top 90 crews were faced with the final 150-mile regularity circuit in the mountains. At that stage Ronnie Adams's Jaguar Mk VII was already in the lead, from Walter Schock's 'works' Mercedes-Benz saloon, and Grosgogeat's DKW. Peter Harper was handily placed, fourth, in his 'works' Sunbeam Mk III, but the next highest 'Brit' was Jimmy Ray, 17th in another 'works' Sunbeam.

The last test, though mountainous, was wet but almost entirely free of snow; as usual there were a few kilometres of the white stuff on top of the Turini. Joan Johns's Austin A90 overturned, Archie Scott-Brown's A50 ran out of brakes and capsized, as did Gerry Burgess's A90 – the BMC team, it seemed, had a lot of development work to do. There were shunts galore, including Peter Harper's assault on a petrol pump at a filling station.

There was no change at the top, for the Ulster crew won comfortably in their 'works' Jaguar Mk VII. Not only did Peter Harper take fourth place, by the way, but Rootes won the Team Prize again. It was almost a British clean sweep.

1956

Starting points from Athens, Glasgow, Lisbon, Munich, Paris, Rome, Stockholm: common route from Paris

    1. R. Adams – F. Biggar   (*Jaguar Mk VIIM*) Glasgow
    2. W. Schock – K. Raebe   (*Mercedes-Benz 220*)
    3. M. Grosgogeat – P. Biagini   (*DKW*)
    4. P. Harper – D. Humphrey   (*Sunbeam Mk III*)
    5. W. Levy – K. Kotott   (*VW Beetle*)
    6. W. Loffler – H. Rathjen   (*BMW 501*)

351 entries, 308 starters, 233 finishers

What happened in 1957?

Plans for the 1957 rally had already been laid when, in October 1956, the Suez crisis erupted. Even though the fighting stopped within days, there was major disruption of petrol supplies for months, with several European countries, including the UK, imposing petrol rationing.

There were to be eight starting points, the concentration point was to be at Chambery, and the final 'shoot-out' was to be over a 150-mile Mountain Circuit taking in the Col du Turini and other familiar Monte Carlo rally territory.

Although entries were accepted from 117 British crews and it was thought that the Monegasques and the French would work out some way of finding enough petrol, the event was finally called off in December 1956, by which time many factory teams had already begun preparation of their cars. Jacques Taffe said that:

'The real reason for the cancellation is psychological. The organisers are afraid that the rally would create jealousy among the French motorists ... We have in fact received permission from the French government to run the rally, and the French Chamber of Commerce was planning for the distribution of petrol ...'

Fortunately, petrol supplies returned to normal in the spring of 1957, so the rally was promoted once again in 1958.

The winner?
The weather!

Perhaps Mother Nature had been saving up for this. A series of mild-weather Montes, then a year off because of petrol rationing, meant that the event was overdue for drama. In 1958 the drama arrived – 303 cars started, but only 59 reached Monte Carlo. Of them, only 38 reached the end of the Mountain Circuit. There was no doubt at all about the result – Monraisse's amazing Dauphine might have taken away most of the trophies, but the weather was the winner.

The organisers dusted off the un-used 1957 route, and used it, unchanged, for 1958. It was to be an altogether simpler event than in 1956, when the Classification Tests had begun in Chambery, with a downhill speed test and a further day's regularity tests used to get a result. The overall distance from starting points to the Mediterranean was down, too, to 1,850 miles, though the Classification Test was no less than 655 miles long. It was almost as if the event had made a pact with the weather – *we* will make it simple, if *you* will make the roads difficult.

As usual, Britain was well represented. There were no fewer than 135 British entrants, and 162 of the 343 entries chose to drive British cars. Ninety-two crews elected to start from Glasgow – then found that the first car would leave at 3.41 a.m. on January 22nd. At least this meant arrival at Barnby Moor for a late lunch, and a Channel crossing during the night.

British 'works' teams were out in strength – four Sunbeam Rapiers from Rootes, four TR3As from Triumph, a mixture of models from BMC (Austin, Morris, MG, Riley and Wolseley were all represented), and seven Zephyrs from Ford.

In 1956 the Italians had objected to making for Taranto before starting towards Monte Carlo, so on this occasion their run-in was drastically changed – in 1958 they had driven all the way past Monte Carlo, through the Massif Central to Montauban before swinging north to St. Claude and starting the serious drive south again! Only nine cars started from this point.

The Classification Test demanded total regularity in certain regions, and in less severe conditions this would have been the talking point. Instead, the awful weather took all the headlines. There was snow all the way from the Glasgow starting point, and for a time the Folkestone-Dover road was blocked; on the run to Dover only London had clear roads. All in all, there is no need for exaggeration – every one of the 59 crews reaching Monte Carlo had been heroic.

After leaving St. Claude, the Paris, Munich and

The Hague starters were decimated in a blizzard, which left only half the event – mainly the Glasgow, Oslo and Lisbon contingent – still running. Only 14 cars reached Villefranche on time from St. Claude, many of the 'works' cars falling by the wayside (literally) in this blizzard-struck area of France; only three crews reached Mauriac on time. The carnage continued once the route struck south through Chambery and Gap, and only the truly professional kept going at all.

When the survivors began to trickle in to Monte Carlo, they looked as if they had been in a war. Fifty-nine made it (22 of them in British cars), but only nine were unpenalised. It is worth noting that they were:

Lycouris (Opel), Jaminon (Simca), Salganick (Panhard), Berger (Simca), Stasse (Borgward), Loffler (Volvo), Cotton (Citroën), Harper (Sunbeam-Rapier) and Gacon (Alfa Romeo).

Monraisse's Renault Dauphine, in 10th place, had a one-minute penalty. Significantly, all except Gacon and Monraisse carried competition numbers between 4 and 31; on this occasion it had been essential to be running at the front, starting from Athens or Oslo, to stand a chance.

The Classification Test – a loop taking in Digne, Gap, Die, Valence, St. Agreve, Nyons and Sisteron – was a day and night race, no more and no less. Only two people could be carried in each car, yet the set average speeds – sometimes at no more than 51 k.p.h./32 m.p.h., but often at 60 k.p.h./37 m.p.h., and sometimes even as high as 70 k.p.h./43 m.p.h. – were more arduous than on any previous event. There were nine long sections, of which Nos. 1 (58 miles), 6 (56 miles) and 8 (28 miles) demanded total regularity. Crews were timed to one-tenth of a second at secret checks, and lost marks heavily if they were early or late.

Fifty-nine crews set out from Monte Carlo at 9 p.m. on the Friday night, but by 3 p.m. on the following day only 38 remained. Three of the nine unpenalised crews disappeared, while the 'works' Renault Dauphine team of Monraisse and Feret overcame a one-minute penalty to forge ahead. Ronnie Adams took a wrong road, Edward Harrison's Ford broke its gearbox, Walter's BMW retired – others lost a lot of time, or ran out of time.

In 655 miles Monraisse's performance was far and away the best of all – he lost 1510 marks compared with Gacon's 2235, and Gatsonides's 2393. The Dutchman, incidentally, started the Test 58th, with huge time penalties, yet made it to sixth place at the finish.

1958

Starting points from Athens, Glasgow, Lisbon, Munich, Oslo, Paris, Rome, The Hague: common route from Saint-Claude

1.	G. Monraisse – J. Feret	(Renault Dauphine) Lisbon
2.	A. Gacon – L. Borsa	(Alfa Romeo Giulietta)
3.	L. Vold-Johansen – F. Koperud	(DKW)
4.	W. Loffler – C. Johansson	(Volvo PV444)
5.	P. Harper – R. Phillips – P. Elbra	(Sunbeam-Rapier)
6.	M. Gatsonides – M. Becquart	(Triumph TR3A)

343 entries, 303 starters, 59 finishers of road section, 38 finishers of mountain circuit

Secret checks controversy; Citroën wins

After the débâcle of 1958, the Monte was run in more predictable weather in 1959. Although there was a great deal of ice and snow on the concentration runs, there was no blizzard and not much fog. But it wasn't a cake-walk – any rally which eliminated Peter Harper and Sydney Allard in accidents had to be treated with respect.

The shadow of 1958, though, still hung over the event a year later. Although the total entry actually increased, there was a shift away from Paris in view of that starting point's elimination in 1958 – 54 cars instead of 91. The most popular starting point – Stockholm (instead of Oslo this time round) – attracted 94 entries. There was also a new start point – Warsaw, well behind the Iron Curtain – which was being used for the first time in post-War years.

Glasgow was chosen by 59 crews, the first of which left in mid-afternoon on January 18th. That meant an evening thrash over the Pennines to the A1, a 2 a.m. departure from the Barnby Moor control, and a morning ferry trip to Boulogne.

South of Chambery strict average speed-keeping was required, with secret checks promised (and figuring very strongly in the results), while the final test was a 270-mile run around the mountains behind Monte Carlo, taking in the Turini, the Col St. Martin, and a long loop out to Castellane and back.

By this time the Monte Carlo rally was not only being followed by every European newspaper and magazine, but by TV and radio stations all over Europe. For them, as for the 'works' teams, it was Big Business, and a great deal of development was going into the car specifications. Tested a year earlier, but more generally available in 1959, was a new breed of tyre, featuring large, tungsten-tipped studs bolted into the treads. These, although crude compared with the 'porcupine' type of the mid-1960s, were thought to be a real breakthrough. In hard-packed snow, and especially on ice, they gave a great deal of grip where none was otherwise available, but at this stage of development they still overheated and caused many punctures. BMC and Standard-Triumph used studded Weathermasters on this occasion; the Rootes Group chose chains but would plump for studded tyres in the future.

Once again British cars were out in force. Nineteen British marques were represented – ranging from a single Berkeley sports car to 24 Jaguars, 23 Fords, 19 Austins and 17 Sunbeams – many of them 'works' supported. BMC entered its usual engaging mixture of models – an A40 Farina for Pat Moss, an MGA Twin-Cam for John Gott, an Austin-Healey Sprite for John Sprinzel, for instance – while Ford built no fewer than eight Zephyrs and Rootes built four Rapiers. Standard-Triumph hedged its bets, with Standard Tens and TR3A sports cars. Renault, on the other hand, withdrew their entries when they decided that the 'secret check' system was going to make this a massive game of chance – they were right.

Even from Stockholm, where wintry weather is guaranteed, the rally got under way well, and it was not until the routes reached central France that the ice and snow began to take its toll. For the crews from six starting points, things got more serious after Aurillac, as the route twisted its way into the Massif Central.

South of Chambery, as expected, the pace became too hot for some. Mary Handley-Page's Rapier slid off the road, Peter Harper pulled over to allow Gatsonides's TR3A go through, and got stuck in deep snow, while Jeff Uren's Zephyr suffered a failed wheel bearing close to the finish. Just 100 yards from the arrival control in Monte Carlo, Gunnar Andersson's Volvo PV544 collided with a local taxi and smashed its front suspension.

It had been tough, but not too tough. Of the 321 starters, 200 reached Monte Carlo, of whom 184 were eligible to tackle the final Mountain Circuit; only 168 actually did so, and 119 finished the event.

So to the Mountain Circuit itself, not as long as that held in 1958, but still complex enough. It was not, however, very demanding on the cars, as the doyen of rallying, John Gott, made clear in his *Autosport* analysis:

'For the classification test skill with a stopwatch was more important than skill with a steering wheel... Constant checking and adjustments of speed were necessary to cope with the threats of secret checks...'

Which would have been fair enough except that his Editor, Gregor Grant, also wrote that:

'I feel perfectly justified in stating quite categorically that unfair methods were adopted [by "fans" of a particular team] in imparting information to certain competitors in the 'Mountains' test. Several cars bearing rally plates and numbers were driven round the opposite way of the circuit and were able to spot the situation of vital [secret] controls.'

Need I say more? In the end Paul Coltelloni (or should I say his navigator Pierre Alexandre?) set the most accurate times, and were adjudged winners. It was all rather unsatisfactory.

1959

Starting points from Athens, Glasgow, Lisbon, Munich, Paris, Rome, Stockholm, The Hague, Warsaw: common route from Chambery

1. P. Coltelloni – P. Alexandre   (*Citroën ID19*) *Paris*
2. A. Thomas – J. Delliere   (*Simca Aronde*)
3. P. Surles – J. Piniers   (*Panhard 850*)
4. H. Marang – J. Badoche   (*Citroën ID19*)
5. R. Adams – E. McMillen   (*Sunbeam-Rapier*)
6. G. Bengtson – C. Lohmander   (*Volvo*)

350 entries, 321 starters, 119 finishers

Deutschland, Deutschland uber alles

There is no other way to describe the 1960 event – it was a complete triumph, a clean sweep for the Mercedes-Benz 'works' team. Not only did the three large silver 220SE saloons take first, second and third places, but they also won the Manufacturers' team prize.

For the British, at least, there was one consolation – Peter Harper, co-driven by BBC motoring correspondent Raymond Baxter, finished fourth overall. Adding this to his fifth place in 1958, and his fourth place in 1956, meant that Harper's unofficial title as 'Ice-master' was secure.

On this event the West Germans took the whole idea of professionalism one stage further. Other teams had practised the rally before Mercedes-Benz joined in, but not to the same extent. Having taken the decision that a good performance on the Mountain Circuit would decide the rally, the team then settled down to practise it, some say for six weeks, some even for two months. It did the trick, for no other team came close. Even so, the winners were not invincible, for they lost time earlier in the event when they found that the Col du Granier was unclimbable without chains.

Compared with 1959 there were no important changes to the routes to Monte Carlo. The common route for all nine columns of competitors began at Chambery, Glasgow starters travelled by Stranraer and Barnby Moor to Dover, and there were high set averages (*and* secret checks) on the route from Chambery to Monte Carlo. Some starting points fared well, and some had it rough, this being due to the way the complex series of routes gradually came together in the Massif Central. Only the Glasgow and Lisbon starters (103 crews) had to tackle the horridly icy and twisting Figeac to Mauriac section – only five were still unpenalised at Chambery, and only 15 qualified to tackle the Mountain Circuit. Fifteen cars started from Athens, but only four cars came out of Yugoslavia, only two cars made it to Monte Carlo.

By the time the routes all joined up at Chambery a great deal of snow, ice, fog (or a combination of all three) had dealt a blow to many hopes. Only 63 cars were still without penalty and this was *before* the high average speed sections even began.

In spite of the uncertainties of the competition, British 'works' teams were numerous – Standard-Triumph sent three TR3As and three of the new Herald Coupés, Rootes sent five Rapiers, BMC sent a fleet of the new front-wheel-drive Minis, while Ford split their forces between new Anglias and disc-braked Zephyrs. As usual they were faced with determined opposition from Volvos, Citroëns, Mercedes-Benz and, for the first time, by Eric Carlsson's Saab.

Even at Chambery some seasoned crews were in trouble, or missing. Nancy Mitchell retired at that point, while Carlsson's Saab took ages to re-start (a faulty coil was eventually discovered). Peter Harper's Rapier had lost nine minutes by getting involved in another crew's accident. Peter Jopp's 'works' Rapier had lost eight minutes by being thwarted by no less than four closed railway crossings.

From Chambery it was a case of ice, ice and more ice. Car after car slid off the road, helpless for lack of grip – even the new-fangled studded tyres had a hard time of it. The Granier was bad, the Gorges de la Bourne was bad, and even the south-facing Còl du Rousset was treacherous. It was all too much for almost everyone. Of the 63 unpenalised cars which left Chambery in the morning, only nine cars were unpenalised when they arrived in Monte Carlo for the first time; one had started from Oslo, one from Glasgow ('Tiny' Lewis's Herald), and seven from Paris. The eventual winner had lost eight minutes, and the second man no less than 19 minutes.

One-hundred-and-fifty-two crews actually reached Monte Carlo, and went off for a night's sleep, but it took ages before the organisers could list which 90 cars were to tackle the Mountain Circuit. Even so, there were angry scenes outside the Permanence as lists were published, then cancelled – even the fourth and final list was eventually agreed to be inaccurate!

The latest version of the Mountain Circuit was a 175-mile loop by way of Piera Cava, the Col du Turini, the Col Saint-Martin, Col de Valberg, Puget-Theniers, Sigale and Pont Charles Albert, which had to be tackled twice; although there was not much snow, a great deal of sand and gravel had been thrown down. this test started at midnight on Saturday, January 23rd, and cars were spaced at two-minute intervals; it was a difficult 12-hour task, where lateness at checks was penalised 60 marks per minute instead of 10 per minute on the run down to the Principality. With an ideal time for each of 12 stages, and with the second run to be at the same speeds as the first, it was a huge challenge.

On the entire Mountain Circuit Walter Schock's error was a mere 30 seconds, while Eugen Bohringer's error was 1 min. 48 sec. Even Peter Harper (with a car-sick Raymond Baxter alongside) lost 10 min. 59 sec. – practice, it seems, had made perfect.

1960

Starting points from Athens, Frankfurt, Glasgow, Lisbon, Oslo, Paris, Rome, The Hague, Warsaw: common route from Chambery

1. *R. Schock – R. Moll* (*Mercedes-Benz 220SE*) *Warsaw*
2. *E. Bohringer – H. Socher* (*Mercedes-Benz 220SE*)
3. *Ott – Mahle* (*Mercedes-Benz 220SE*)
4. *P. Harper – R. Baxter* (*Sunbeam-Rapier*)
5. *Tak – Swaab* (*Mercedes-Benz 220SE*)
6. *M. Sutcliffe – P. Crabtree* (*Ford Zephyr II*)

345 entries, 311 starters, 152 finishers

Part 3:
Special stages at last – the Monte as a speed event

Special stages, but a weird handicap!

The Monte Carlo rally organisers were nothing if not reactionary. For 1961 they reacted to years of criticism, and changed the format of the event – but hung on to the old traditions. This might have been the first Monte to include flat-out speed tests, but it was still dominated by a handicap, perhaps the most controversial of all time. The other novelty was that Anthony Noghes had retired, Louis Chiron taking his place.

After the eight routes had converged on Charbonnieres (survivors of the 13 Athens starters would be the last to join in), there was to be a 450-mile run through the mountains to Monte Carlo. Along the way there were five special stages, all at heights of more than 800 metres/2,500 feet, which meant that ice and snow was virtually assured. The longest – the St. Auban, and Col du Turini stages – kept competitors racing for up to 40 minutes at a time, while the shortest (up to Peille, at the back of Mont Agel) was a seven- or eight-minute blast. Short time trials around the Monaco GP circuit were re-introduced, to sort out the final positions.

This, on the surface, was fair enough – except that the organisers insisted on imposing a handicap (or 'Factor of Comparison') which would be used to 'equate' the stage times achieved by all the cars. This favoured heavy cars with small engines, Group One cars against Group Two cars, and penalised two-stroke machines. A little slide-rule work showed that the French Panhard PL17s had much the most favourable 'Factor' – which led the cynics to suggest that it was Panhard's 'turn to win'. *Autosport*'s noted analyst, John Gott, quite simply called this 'Biased'.

As usual, the organisers were not prepared to admit that they had (a) made any mistakes or (b) favoured a particular type of car. The 'works' teams had to grin and bear it. Saab sent Eric Carlsson in a 95 estate, not only because it was heavier, but because it had a four-speed gearbox. Rootes sent their Rapiers with three-men crews. Others wrote off their chances before they even started. And why not? – on the last 6 km. stage the Panhards could be 1 min. 12 sec. slower than Mini-Minors, and nearly 2 mins. slower than Porsche coupés, yet still 'beat' them on handicap. On the longest stage the Porsches needed to be *nine minutes* faster to 'beat' them.

In spite of this entry – at 346 cars, 305 of which started – was as high as ever. No fewer than 110 entries came from the UK (many more than this had applied), of which 66 elected to start from Glasgow, 16 from Paris and 14 from Stockholm. The Swedish capital, in fact, was the most popular of all, with 98 entrants, the least popular being Frankfurt (15) and Athens (13 – the weather in Yugoslavia was a great deterrent).

As in 1960, the core of the routes was a circular tour of France, this time with a Monte Carlo start being re-instated. It was Stockholm's turn to host the Scandinavian start point, while the poorly-supported Rome and The Hague start points of 1960 had been abandoned. Glasgow starters went via Stranraer, and Barnby Moor, to Dover, and across the Channel to Boulogne.

In spite of the unfairly balanced handicap, there was still a great deal of interest from 'works' teams. Ford entered Anglias and one Zephyr, BMC entered A40s and Mini-Minors and Rootes prepared a fleet of Rapiers; Standard-Triumph gave the event a miss. Panhard, naturally, entered a team, as did Mercedes-Benz and Saab. BBC TV sank to a new low by entering a London taxi, as a gimmick, with Tony Brooks and Willy Cave driving, and with the meter running all the time.

The run in to Charbonnieres was in relatively mild weather, though all but three of the Glasgow starters lost time in the Jura, and only 199 cars re-started from Charbonnieres. With the accent on speed thereafter another 40 competitors dropped out on the run down to Monte Carlo. Eighty-four cars were still 'clean' on the road sections at the finish.

The Athens route was particularly mild – which was something of a miracle in view of that route's fearsome reputation.

Let's forget that a Panhard win was inevitable (the cars were awarded first, second and third places – even though M. Martin's car finished 13 min. 37 sec. 'off the pace' on actual stage times), and concentrate on the actual stage times. The moral victor was Rene Trautmann (Citroën DS19), who was fastest on three of the five stages, and second fastest on another – he was 2 min. 21 sec. clear of Carlsson's Saab Estate car; even so he was handicapped down to 19th overall... Gunnar Andersson's Volvo was third 'on scratch', with Pauli Toivonen's Citroën fourth and Jean Rolland's Citroën fifth. Paddy Hopkirk's Sunbeam-Rapier was 'best Brit', in ninth.

The Monaco GP test, where the fastest of four laps was itself 'handicapped' to carry the same importance as a 30 km. special stage, saw the third Panhard improve from sixth to third place – it also saw Mike Parkes's Rapier hit the wall when a wheel broke up, while Bohringer's Mercedes-Benz 220SE also lost a wheel as it completed the course.

Like most of that year's event, farce rather than high drama was the keynote. 1962 could only be better.

1961

The first Monte Carlo to use special stages: starting points from Athens, Frankfurt, Glasgow, Lisbon, Monte Carlo, Paris, Stockholm, Warsaw: common route from Charbonnieres

1. M. Martin – R. Bateau (Panhard Tigre) Monte Carlo
2. W. Loffler – H. Walter (Panhard Tigre)
3. G. Jouanneaux – A. Coquillet (Panhard Tigre)
4. E. Carlsson – K. Svensson (Saab 95 Estate)
5. K. Block – H. Paul (BMW 700)
6. E. Keinanen – R. Eklund (Skoda Octavia)

346 entries, 305 starters, 156 finishers

Victory for Carlsson's 2-stroke Saab

Although there was still a handicap to be surmounted, the 1962 event was much better received than that of 1961. The January weather was extraordinarily mild (although the stages were still snow-covered), and the best car-driver combinations headed the lists.

Except that Oslo took its turn to start off the cars from Scandinavia, and that all routes joined up at St. Claude, the rally looked very similar to 1961. The 'Factor of Comparison' was dependent on a car's engine size, and its Appendix J grouping – this gave Sunbeam-Rapier a 'factor' of 0.339 compared with a Group Two Mini-Cooper's 0.342, and a Group Two Saab's 0.341. GT or Group Three cars were penalised by about six per cent compared with normal production vehicles. Certainly there was no pre-destined result before the rally began.

This time around, the 65 Glasgow starters had to travel 2,513 miles to reach Monte Carlo, and the British route was by way of a control at Banbury (the first time that town had ever figured in a Monte Carlo route). A vaccination scare before the start, in Glasgow, had been solved by Dr. Alex Mitchell, a competitor who then had the cruel luck to crash on the way from Scotch Corner to Banbury – it was not the first time that Dr. Mitchell had failed to get out of England on his way to Monte Carlo.

If the weather had not been so mild, many more cars would have lost time in the *Massif Central*, but as it happened almost all crews had time for leisurely meals, not to say time for sight-seeing, on route.

Even though rallying's 'professionals', were on the march, with lengthy recces now considered normal for this event, with service cars and tyre choice proliferating, the number of true private owners held up remarkably well. No fewer than 313 cars started, with 247 of them reaching the finish.

The hard motoring began from Chambery and, as in 1961, there were five special stages between there and Monte Carlo. In later years these would all be seen as 'classics' – we now know them as the Granier, Mont Ventoux, Quatres Chemins, St. Auban 2 (down 'the chute') and the Col du Turini, with the Granier longest of all at 45 kms.

To round off everything, there was a speed trial around the Monaco GP circuit; afterwards, as usual, there was to be an optional driving test held on the quayside.

Apart from the well-established rally cars, this was also the first appearance of BMC's Mini-Coopers, one of which was driven by a young Finn called Rauno Aaltonen; BMC's team, of course, was

A privateers' battle – Norman Blockley's Austin A40 'Farina' (which had started from Warsaw), being caught by the Eklund-Eklund Skoda, which had started from Oslo.

under new management: Stuart Turner had vacated his co-driving seat with Eric Carlsson to succeed Marcus Chambers as competitions manager.

This was the first Monte in which scratch times were almost (if not quite) enough to produce the rally winners. On the first long stage (the Cols du Granier, Cucheron and Porte, south of Chambery), Eric Carlsson's Saab recorded 40 min. 27 sec., but Peter Procter's 'works' Rapier would surely have beaten him if he had not punctured and had to change a wheel in mid-stage.

Up Mont Ventoux, to the junction, Walter's Porsche Carrera recorded 10 min. 05 sec. to set fastest time, followed by Siegle-Morris's Austin-Healey 3000, and with Bohringer's big Mercedes-Benz 220SE beating the Rapiers (Hopkirk, Harper and Procter), which in turn all beat the Saab. The same drivers, with permutations, dominated the last three stages.

Rauno Aaltonen, sharing the 'works' Mini-Cooper with Geoff Mabbs, was eliminated on the descent of the Turini when he crashed the car, but the car had made a promising start – we would see much of the Mini-Cooper family in the next few Monte Carlo rallies!

According to *actual* times on the special stages (with no 'Factor of Comparison' added), Carlsson's Saab had beaten Bohringer's Mercedes-Benz saloon by a mere five seconds, with Walter's Group Three Porsche a further 67 seconds back, and Messrs. Hopkirk, Seigle-Morris, Neyret (Citroën), Procter and Morley (MGA) behind them. The Porsche and the Austin-Healey, of course, had no chance of beating their handicaps.

By the time the four-lap circuit test had been run, Carlsson's screaming little Saab was indeed confirmed as the victor, from Bohringer's 220SE, though Paddy Hopkirk rose to third place, and Procter's sister Rapier to fourth. Because Peter Harper finished 12th (and Grand Prix driver Graham Hill finished 10th in another 'works' Rapier), it was no surprise for Rootes to win the Manufacturers' Team prize as well.

As usual, John Gott, writing in *Autosport*, summed up accurately by writing that:

> 'The 31st Rally... cannot be rated as a great event, but it was more intelligently planned and far better organised than any recent "Monte"...'

And as the same magazine's Editor, Gregor Grant, summarised:

> 'So it was all over, and no one could grumble about the result, for Carlsson and his Saab had been outstanding in every way.'

1962

Starting points from Athens, Frankfurt, Glasgow, Lisbon, Monte Carlo, Oslo, Paris, Warsaw: common route from St. Claude

1. E. Carlsson – G. Haggbom (Saab 96) Oslo
2. E. Bohringer – P. Lang (Mercedes-Benz 220SE)
3. P. Hopkirk – J. Scott (Sunbeam-Rapier)
4. P. Procter – G. Robson (Sunbeam-Rapier)
5. P. Gele – A. Guilhaudin (DKW)
6. G. Andersson – W. Karlsson (Volvo)

351 entries, 313 starters, 247 finishers

Carlsson's Saab beats the blizzards

Even before the 1963 event started the combination of Eric Carlsson/Saab 96 was freely tipped for victory. In the previous two years the giant Swede had been so successful, in so many types of event, that he was considered unbeatable on snow and ice. If the bookmakers had been involved, they would have had a hard time. Carlsson was a 'racing certainty' – and won, comfortably.

Compared with 1962 the weather was terrible, with something approaching blizzard conditions obliterating the route from St. Claude to Monte Carlo. The statistics tell their own story – 296 cars started, but only 216 remained by the time the convoy left Chambery for the first special stage. Less than half of these stalwarts – 102 to be precise – made it to Monte Carlo.

The route itself was similar to that used in 1962, this time with Stockholm hosting the 84-strong Scandinavian contingent. There were 65 Glasgow starters who had to clock in at controls in Melrose and at the Belfry Hotel, Wishaw, near Sutton Coldfield, before making for Dover. As so often before, the Channel crossing was at dead of night, with continental motoring beginning from Boulogne at 6.50 a.m. on the second day.

The 'meat' of the event was five special stages, the longest being over the Cols du Granier, Cucheron and Porte, the fastest being up Mont Ventoux, and the highest being up and over the Col du Turini. To round it off there were speed trials around the Monaco GP circuit.

More and more 'works' teams were involved, and the mountains behind Monte Carlo were buzzing with practice cars for several weeks. Adding to the Ford, BMC and Rootes teams was a Standard-Triumph entry of three Vitesses and a TR4, and a team of Reliant Sabres. Not only that, but Ford-USA entered a team of lightweight Falcon Sprints (to be driven by Bo Ljungfeldt, Peter Jopp, and Anne Hall) – their pre-event publicity made it clear that they expected to win!

All the serious European teams were involved, of which the 'works' Saabs, Volvos, Mercedes-Benz and Citroëns were best fancied. As usual, hundreds of hopeful private owners entered, to make their annual pilgrimage to the wintry sun over the Moyenne Corniche.

As in 1962, there was a complex 'Factor of Comparison' to be applied to all cars' stage times. For Group One (production cars) this factor was:

$$r = \sqrt{\frac{C}{8C+1}}$$

– where C was the car's engine capacity in litres. Group Two cars had that factor multiplied by 1.03, and Group Three (GT cars) by 1.06. GT cars, in other words, were handicapped by six per cent. Although there was still a small bias towards smaller engined cars, it was as equitable a handicapping system as the Monte Carlo rally had ever applied, and most teams were happy to live with it.

Right from the start, weather (and road) conditions on the continent were awful. Blockages on German autobahns meant that cars had to go 'the long way round' – Peter Harper's Rapier completed an extra 154 miles and averaged 76 m.p.h., to reach Bad Driburg from Frankfurt. The 13 Athens starters were marooned by heavy snow storms in Jugoslavia. Almost all the Monte Carlo starters lost time on the very first night. Belgian, Dutch, and French roads were skating rinks, and even the latest in studded tyre technology was hard-pressed to keep cars on the road.

The latest studded tyres, incidentally, came from Scandinavia, and featured hundreds of small 'pin' studs in all-weather treads, rather than the large tungsten-tipped spikes used in the British variety.

When fresh, such tyres produced so much grip that it was possible to encourage brake fade on hard-packed snow in under-braked cars!

On the 500 mile run from Chambery to Monte Carlo, there were driving heroics on the so-called 'road' sections as well as on the stages. It was the sort of night which left many cars in ditches, wrapped around trees, on snow banks, or down ravines; no-one, fortunately, was hurt.

The most spectacular of all on the special stages was Bo Ljungfeldt, in his 4.2 litre engined Ford Falcon; he was faster overall, than the diminutive Saab of Eric Carlsson. Unhappily, though, he had lost time in the hold-ups north of Monte Carlo on that awful first night, and was right out of contention. On the Monaco circuit, Hans Walter's Porsche Carrera was fastest, with Makinen's Austin-Healey 3000 and Thuner's Triumph TR4 close behind.

As expected, Eric Carlsson won the event, but let's never forget Pauli Toivonen's stirring performance in the big Citroën, and Rauno Aaltonen's fine third place in a 997cc-engined Mini-Cooper. All three had started from Stockholm. Front-wheel-drive had dominated the results – and the Mini-Cooper challenge was maturing. It promised to be quite a race in 1964.

1963

Starting points from Athens, Frankfurt, Glasgow, Lisbon, Monte Carlo, Paris, Stockholm, Warsaw: common route from St. Claude.

    1. *E. Carlsson – G. Palm*   *(Saab 96) Stockholm*
    2. *P. Toivonen – A. Jarvi*   *(Citroën ID19)*
    3. *R. Aaltonen – A. Ambrose*   *(BMC Mini-Cooper)*
    4. *L. Bianchi – J-C. Ogier*   *(Citroën ID19)*
    5. *R. Neyret*
      – J. Terramorsi   *(Citroën ID19)*
    6. *P. Hopkirk – J. Scott*   *(BMC Mini-Cooper)*

341 entries, 296 starters, 102 finishers

Hopkirk victorious – the start of the Mini years

Every year the Monte had its own particular character. In 1964, no doubt, it was the 'Year of the Mini'. Although there would be even cleaner sweeps in the years to come, the BMC performance in 1964 was emphatic enough for people to realise that a new era had arrived.

By this time, of course, Mini-Minor had given way to Mini-Cooper, and Mini-Cooper S had elbowed both of them aside. All over Europe the 10 ft. long red-painted 'works' cars had started winning rallies – not just on handicap, and not just in their class, but outright. Front-wheel-drive, professional drivers, dedicated mechanics and an all-seeing competitions manager (Stuart Turner) all made a contribution.

To combat the phalanx of Mini-Coopers, Ford entered several Cortina GTs, Rootes entered rear-engined Imps and old-type Rapiers, Reliant entered Sabre Six coupés, while Ford-USA entered no fewer than eight of their re-styled 4.7 litre Falcon Futura Sprint coupés. Among the Falcon drivers, this time round, were Ljungfeldt, Graham Hill, Peter Harper, Anne Hall, Peter Jopp, and Henri Greder. As usual, Carlsson had a two-stroke Saab, Eugen Bohringer had a Mercedes-Benz 220SE and there was a positive fleet of Citroëns.

Compared with 1963, route changes were minimal. For the first time in many years a Russian start point (Minsk) was chosen, though this was poorly patronised. Twenty-nine crews nominated Minsk, only five of them from the Soviet Union itself. On this occasion the Glasgow entry had dropped to 37 (perhaps the horrors of 1963 finally convinced some amateurs to stay at home?), and the British route went by way of Llandrindod Wells, New Milton (near Bournemouth), and Dover, with the Channel crossing actually in the evening, rather than during the night.

Except that the 'handicap' for Group Two cars was increased to four per cent and that for Group Three cars *reduced* to five per cent, there were no changes in the 'Factor of Comparison' rating, which encouraged factory teams like BMC to concentrate on Group Two cars, though the Morley twins were sent out to win the GT category in an MGA, which they duly did.

If 1963's weather had annihilated many hopes, that of 1964 was extremely mild, boring for the drivers, and easy to deal with. Two-hundred-and-twenty-five of the 299 starters reached the start of the *Route Commun* at Rheims, where there was an hour's break. Conditions were still good to Gerardmer, where many cars had an hour in hand, but by the time Chambery was reached the tempo had hotted up, and the snow and ice was evident, at least on higher ground.

Thereafter, it was not easy. One-hundred-and-sixty-seven cars managed to finish, but by the time they reached Monte Carlo only 73 were unpenalised on the road section – and there was still the Monaco GP test to go!

The 'flat-out' section of the 1964 event followed that established in 1961 – there were to be five special stages, and a final sprint around the Monaco GP circuit. The stages themselves, however, were mainly new. The first started from St. Disdier, in the mountains north of Gap, and snaked over the Col du Festre, while the second climbed over the Col d'Espreaux, flashed through Barcillonnette and Sigoyer, and ended on the outskirts of Gap. The third stage circled a huge new reservoir east of Gap, before the final two stages included an old favourite, the assault on the Col du Turini in the usual West-East direction; only 7 km. of that 23 km. stage, incidentally were snow covered.

By 1964 every 'works' crew would have practised these stages assiduously in the weeks before the event, so the speeds achieved on special stages were mind-boggling. Scandinavians like Eric Carlsson, Timo Makinen and Bo Ljungfeldt not only had skilled navigators to read the pace-notes over to them on helmet-to-helmet intercom systems, but they had actually committed all the twists and turns to memory.

Top speeds of more than 100 m.p.h., sometimes on ice and snow but sometimes on bare roads, with studded tyres, were quite normal. It was a far cry from the heroic pre-War days of the Monte Carlo rally where grip was gained by strap-on chains, and where a top speed of 60 m.p.h. was considered very daring indeed.

There was no doubt that the Falcons were quicker than ever – and this year there was no disappointment due to lost time at an earlier stage. Because they had large engines, however, they suffered somewhat from the 'Factor' – and on arrival in Monte Carlo the amazing Ljungfeldt was in fourth place.

Before the circuit test Paddy Hopkirk's 1,071cc Mini-Cooper S was in the lead, chased by the two 'works' Saabs of Eric Carlsson and his wife Pat Moss-Carlsson (already famous, under her maiden name, as Pat Moss, of course). On the circuit,

Noted journalist Michael Frostick not only wrote about the rally, but found time to compete in it too. In 1964 he drove a 'works' Hillman Imp, starting from Minsk in Russia, while...

Ljungfeldt was no less than 40 sec. quicker than Carlsson in three flying laps – good enough to lift him to second place. In the same way, Timo Makinen elbowed his way past Pat Moss-Carlsson, who finished fifth overall.

The 'works' BMC Mini-Coopers took first, fourth and seventh places – so naturally they won the Team Prize too. It would be an even more emphatic victory in 1965.

1964

Starting points from Athens, Frankfurt, Glasgow, Lisbon, Minsk, Monte Carlo, Oslo, Paris, Warsaw: common route from Rheims.

1. *P. Hopkirk – H. Liddon*   *(BMC Mini-Cooper S) Minsk*
2. *B. Ljungfeldt – F. Sager*   *(Ford Falcon Sprint)*
3. *E. Carlsson – G. Palm*   *(Saab 96)*
4. *T. Makinen – P. Vanson*   *(BMC Mini-Cooper S)*
5. *Ms. P. Moss-Carlsson – Ms. U. Wirth*   *(Saab 96)*
6. *T. Trana – S. Lindstrom*   *(Volvo 120 Series)*

342 entries, 299 starters, 167 finishers

1965

Timo Makinen and the unstoppable Cooper S

This was the year in which the Monte almost, but not quite fell into line with other world-class rallies. The Monaco GP circuit test was scrapped in favour of extra special stages, and the 'Factor of Comparison' was watered down yet further. The organisers were still not ready to make this truly a scratch event, but it was getting closer all the time.

For the organisers and the hoteliers of the Principality, the bad news was that rally entries were trending sharply downwards. Compared with 1964 there were 67 fewer entries – 274 compared with 341 – and this trend would continue in the next few years. As the rally became faster and more serious, the 'works' teams became dominant, while more and more private entrants realised that they were wasting their time – and a considerable amount of money – in merely making up the numbers.

There was an impressive line-up of 'works' teams, from BMC, Ford, Rootes, Triumph, Rover, Saab, Citroën – and even from Porsche, who sent Eugen Bohringer in a 904 Coupé, which was nothing less than a full-house racing sports car! Interesting new rally cars included the nimble Rover 2000s (for whom a youthful Roger Clark was the star driver), and the powerful Sunbeam Tiger sports car, driven on this occasion by Peter Harper and Andrew Cowan.

The hoteliers did not lose out completely though. Bigger works teams, with more mechanics, service crews, and allied staff, swelled the numbers considerably – it was still mighty difficult to find a room in Monte Carlo unless one had booked months in advance!

On this occasion there were 76 British entries – and although this exceeded that of any other country it was a far cry from the heady days of the 1950s when upwards of 400 fought for the privilege of doing this event. For 49 of them, who chose to start from the UK, there was a major route change. The Glasgow start had been abandoned, along with its tedious run down the country. Instead, the start was from Duke of York's Barracks in London, after which 2 hr. 43 min. was allowed for the drive to Dover, ahead of the usual cross-Channel trip to Boulogne. The first London starter left at the unearthly time of 03.26 hrs . . .

There were two 'arms' to the concentration runs. The same basic circular tour of France, and the same trundle across Eastern Europe were used, with all routes getting together at St. Claude. Then, from Chambery, there was a 500 mile, 14 hr. 30 min., dash over the mountains to Monte Carlo, taking in five

. . . In 1965 he shared the work with Maxwell Boyd, and borrowed a 'works' Ford Corsair GT.

In 1965 Timo Makinen's BMC Mini-Cooper S obliterated all opposition, but Peter Harper and Ian Hall provided much excitement in their 200 b.h.p. Sunbeam Tiger, and finished fourth overall.

special stages.

After a night's sleep, the 120 best-placed finishers were then asked to tackle an even tougher 379 Mountain Circuit to and from Monte Carlo, which was to cover a complex cat's-cradle of mountain roads in the *Alpes Maritimes*, and six special stages, including two passages of the Turini and two of the Col de Couillole. It was the sort of night which, even in good weather, would tax a driver's stamina, and a 'works' team's resources, to the limit.

By looking back at the weather history of this event, it was clear that another awful year was due. Before the cars all reached St. Claude the wintry conditions were bearable, but once the cars pointed their noses uphill from Chambery the ice, and in particular the falling snow, arrived with a vengeance.

The 47 km. Granier stage was bad enough, with every possible combination of surfaces, the Chamrousse section (not a stage in previous years) was worse, and as the cars fought their way towards the Mediterranean the blizzard conditions intensified. Dozens of famous 'works' crews went off the road, lost time, or suffered car breakdowns – even the Eric Carlsson/Saab combination losing nearly an hour with engine trouble. Vic Elford, Terry Hunter, Paddy Hopkirk and the Morleys all crashed.

Throughout the night, it was a rout, as the vast majority of the field was eliminated. By the time the *Arrivée* control on the quayside had closed, a mere 35 of the 211 cars which left St. Claude were still running, and qualified as finishers; this had come as close to a complete 'white-out' as any previous rally had ever done.

Only one car – the BMC Mini-Cooper 1275S of Timo Makinen – had lost no time on the road sections, and he was also much the fastest (by a staggering *eight minutes*) over about 120 minutes of stages! Lucien Bianchi's Citroën DS19 had lost two minutes, and the astonishing Bohringer's Porsche 904 had lost four minutes, with only Neyret (Citroën) and Peter Harper (Sunbeam Tiger) also under ten minutes late.

The Mountain Circuit merely emphasised Makinen's complete dominance of this rally (his stage time total was 4½ minutes in the clear of anyone else), while behind him there was a minor reshuffle of places. The unfortunate Bianchi crashed out of the event, while two of the three Triumph Spitfires expired with engine trouble. Bohringer eased the squat Porsche into second place ahead of Pat Moss-Carlsson's Saab 96 Sport, while the imperturbable Roger Clark took sixth *and* won the Group One category in his Rover 2000. Just 22 crews completed the whole route.

1965

Starting points from Athens, Frankfurt, Lisbon, London, Minsk, Monte Carlo, Paris, Stockholm, Warsaw: common route from St. Claude.

1.	T. Makinen – P. Easter	(BMC Mini-Cooper S) Stockholm
2.	E. Bohringer – R. Wutherich	(Porsche 904)
3.	Ms. P. Moss-Carlsson – Ms. E. Nystrom	(Saab 96)
4.	P. Harper – I. Hall	(Sunbeam Tiger)
5.	H. Linge – P. Falk	(Porsche 911)
6.	R. Clark – J. Porter	(Rover 2000)

274 entries, 237 starters, 35 finishers

The 'Lighting Fiasco'

This was the year in which the rally lost a lot of credibility. Not only did the organisers impose a formula guaranteed to hand victory to a Group One (showroom-tune) car, but they found what many observers believed to be a trumped-up excuse to disqualify the three 'works' BMC Mini-Cooper S saloons which dominated the event.

As ever with the Monte Carlo organisers, it was best not to analyse their reasoning – before, during or after the event. Some say they were unhappy that 'homologation specials' now held the initiative, and some say that they thought French cars might have a chance if the competition was restricted to Group One cars. Others say...no, we'd better not go further.

For 1966, the regulations used Group One as the 'base' for the event. Any competitor using modified (Group Two or Group Three) cars would suffer an 18 per cent time penalty on the special stages. Well before the event, my *Autocar* rally guide commented that: 'Most competition managers are convinced that the rally will be won and lost at scrutineering on Friday next...' If only I had known how much heartache there would be!

Although the total entry was down yet again, as ever there was massive support from the 'works'

teams. BMC, Ford, Rootes, Standard-Triumph and Rover all entered British teams. Saab and Volvo both abstained, but Citroën and Lancia were present in force. There were 50 British entrants, 37 of them electing to start from the Excelsior Hotel at London Airport.

The concentration runs were straightforward enough, this time with only nine cars from Athens and four from Minsk. On Monday, January 17th, all surviving crews faced a 24 hour/900 mile *Parcours Commun* across the mountains to and from Chambery, which included six special stages (one being cancelled before the day, one being the Granier, of course...). Then, on the Wednesday night, the top sixty tackled the 380 mile Mountain Circuit, which included six stages, three of which were up-and-over assaults on the Col du Turini.

BMC, as ever, was well prepared, for it achieved Group One homologation of the Mini-Cooper S, this including twin fuel tanks and an engine cooler. Not only that, but team manager Stuart Turner had invented the philosophy of 'ice notes' crews, who would drive over the stages just before the French police closed the roads, modifying competitors' pace notes to show where the hazards had changed; this strategy, in fact, was going to be critical to their

Rover came into rallying in the early 1960s, and entered several 'showroom-standard' 2000 models in the 1965 and 1966 events. In 1965 Roger Clark drove the sister car to this example (registered 4 KUE) to victory in the Group 1 category.

performance.

One-hundred-and-sixty-four of the original 192 starters reached Monte Carlo, 130 of them still with clean sheets. The pace on the next 24-hour run was hot, with many 'works' cars forced out by crashes. Eighty-eight crews made it back to Monte Carlo, 39 of them still 'clean' on the road. At this point British teams dominated the standings – Makinen (Mini-

Cooper S), Aaltonen (Mini-Cooper S), Ljungfeldt (Lotus-Cortina), R. Clark (Lotus-Cortina), and Hopkirk (Mini-Cooper S) in that order. The best 'works' Citroën was Pauli Toivonen in seventh place, with Munari's Lancia Flavia eighth. The Minis had actually beaten Gunter Klass's Porsche 911 on several stages . . .

Even before the Mountain Circuit, the British

The 'works' BMC Mini-Coopers were always competitive, and celebrated three victories (1964, 1965 and 1967) and were disqualified from victory in 1966. This was Tony Fall's car in the 1967 event, carrying some of the compulsorily marked tyres on the roof rack, a feature of the 'handicap' on that year's rally.

cars were carefully scrutineered, and 'inefficacity' (sic) in their lights was pointed out. Trouble in store . . .

On the last night, which included three stirring passages over the Turini, BMC tightened its grip on the ice and snow, for Paddy Hopkirk moved up to third. Only Ljungfeldt (who crashed his car near Moulinet) had to retire. With Roger Clark's Lotus-

Cortina in fourth place it looked like a clean sweep for the Brits.

Then the aggravation began. No-one was willing to admit that they had protested against the British cars, but the BMC Minis were painstakingly stripped, to their last nut and bolt. The organisers, it seemed, could not see how a Mini could beat a Porsche (a Group Three Porsche, no less), nor how such cars could be faster than *all* the French Citroëns and Italian Lancias. The fact that the BMC cars had practised well, had the significant advantage of 'ice-notes' crews, and had the world's best drivers, didn't seem to matter.

In the end the organisers triumphantly said that the British cars lighting systems did not comply with French law (the fact that the Citroëns had been seen using white lights was not even taken into considera-tion...), and disqualified them all. BMC lost its One-Two-Three finish, Roger Clark his fourth place, and Rosemary Smith (Hillman Imp) her Ladies' Prize. No amount of appealing – to reason *or* to higher authority – could change all that.

Pauli Toivonen's Citroën, therefore, was awarded the outright win; perhaps it is significant that he never again drove for the French team – he didn't have the gall to win any more rallies that way.

1966

The 'Group One' event: starting points from Athens, Bad Hombourg, Lisbon, London, Minsk, Monte Carlo, Oslo, Rheims, Warsaw: common route from arrival in Monte Carlo.

**1. P. Toivonen – E. Mikander (Citroën DS21) Oslo
   2. R. Trautmann –
       J. Hanrioud (Lancia Flavia Coupé)
   3. O. Andersson
      – O. Dahlgren (Lancia Flavia Coupé)
   4. R. Neyret – J. Terramorsi (Citroën DS21)
   5. L. Cella – L. Lombardini (Lancia Fulvia)
   6. R. Slotemaker – R. Gorris (BMW 2000)

242 entries, 192 starters, 164 finishers

** *Before disqualifications the position was:*

    1. T. Makinen – P. Easter (BMC Mini-Cooper S)
   2. R. Aaltonen – A. Ambrose) (BMC Mini-Cooper S)
   3. P. Hopkirk – H. Liddon) (BMC Mini-Cooper S)
    4. R. Clark – J. Porter (Ford Cortina-Lotus Mk I)
  5. P. Toivonen – E. Mikander (Citroën DS21)
  6. R. Trautmann – J. Hanrioud (Lancia Flavia Coupé)

Vindication for BMC

After the shambles of the 1966 event, it was a miracle that entries held up so well in 1967; there were 13 fewer entries than in the previous year, though British interest had plummeted from 53 to 35 crews. Not only that, but there were no 'works' entries from Ford, Rover, or Triumph. BMC, at least, had a point to prove, turning up with no fewer than five 1.3 litre Mini-Cooper Ss. Their major rivals included Lancia, Porsche, and Renault – it was Vic Elford's first Porsche drive, and much was expected of him.

Although the route was much as before, there was yet another new handicapping system. Category One cars ran off scratch, but there was also a Category Two, where cars were only able to use eight tyres *in total* on each of the long Monte Carlo-Monte Carlo loops; in exchange for this limitation, their time penalties would be multiplied by 0.88 (in fact, therefore, they would be reduced by 12 per cent).

Theoretically Category Two was meant to make the rally more attractive to impecunious private owners. In fact it meant that all the factory teams did their sums, consulted their tyre suppliers, arranged to have an even wider choice of rubber, tread patterns, and studding arrangements than ever – and entered in Category Two!

The British starting point finally reached Dover (it could go no further without being abandoned completely), and the Minsk start was abandoned; Dover, Frankfurt, Rheims and Monte Carlo itself were the most popular starting places, with Dover starters having the lowest numbers of all. BMC spread its starters – Athens, Dover, Lisbon and Monte Carlo – reasoning that one team, at least, would get the best of the weather in the mountains.

Except for the Athens competitors, the concentration runs to Monte Carlo were extremely easy, with 167 cars qualifying to continue. This meant that everything would hinge on the six-stage/21½-hour/800 mile *Parcours Commun*, and on the six-stage/11 hour/380 mile Mountain Circuit, the latter only to be tackled by the top sixty crews.

Last minute practice before the *Parcours Commun* revealed spring-like conditions in the mountains, which made tyre choice very difficult indeed. Mont Ventoux was almost completely dry, while even the famous Granier/Cucheron/Porte special stage was three-quarters clear of ice and snow. In such conditions the Minis struggled to keep ahead, with Elford's Porsche, Munari's and Ove Andersson's Lancia Fulvia HFs, and the Renault Gordini 1300s all getting into the top ten on stages. Elford, in fact, was fastest on three of the six stages, and at the end of the 800 mile loop he led three Mini-Cooper S cars (37 seconds ahead of Paddy Hopkirk, who was closely followed by Timo Makinen and Rauno Aaltonen); 101 cars made it back to the parking area on the harbour front.

The top sixty then had a night in bed before tackling the mountain circuit. This time there was more snow, and a lot more fell during the night. Clearly this would favour the front-wheel-drive cars – but what no-one had forecast was how well the 'works' Lancias would perform.

On such a night Elford's Porsche was always in trouble, and it eventually slipped back to third place. Timo Makinen's Mini-Cooper S then led, until it hit a huge rock in the road on one of the road sections; there were dark rumours about sabotage, but these were discounted. Rauno Aaltonen passed Paddy Hopkirk and looked to be an easy victor.

Except that Ove Andersson's Lancia caught up rapidly. He had been 65 seconds behind Aaltonen when the night began, but was only 13 seconds behind at the finish. In the last two special stages he

had beaten Aaltonen by 44 seconds – one more stage on fresh snow might have been enough...

Of the 60 which started the final night, 40 were running at the end; 15 of these were British drivers, and 20 of them were British cars. Somehow, it all made up for 1966.

For BMC it was the vindication of everything they thought had been achieved in the previous year; team cars had now finished first on the rally on four consecutive occasions, and officially been recorded as winners on three of them.

Once again the organisers' handicap system failed to level 'works' and private entries, for in the tyre-limited Category Two no private entrant got a look in. There were three factory Minis, three Lancias, three Renault Gordinis and Elford's Porsche in the top ten! Category One, the 'scratch' formula, was a low key affair, with 'works' Citroën DS21s finishing first and second (Robert Neyret and J-C. Ogier). Renault were quite happy, for they won the manufacturers' team prize, and Sylvia Osterberg used a Gordini 1300 to win the Ladies' prize.

1967

Starting points from Athens, Dover, Frankfurt, Lisbon, Monte Carlo, Oslo, Rheims, Warsaw: common route from arrival in Monte Carlo.

    1. R Aaltonen – H. Liddon   (BMC Mini-Cooper S) Monte Carlo
2. O. Andersson – J. Davenport   (Lancia Fulvia HF)
   3. V. Elford – D. Stone   (Porsche 911S)
   4. L. Cella – L. Lombardini   (Lancia Fulvia HF)
   5. S. Munari – G. Harris   (Lancia Fulvia HF)
   6. P. Hopkirk – R. Crellin   (BMC Mini-Cooper S)

229 entries, 195 starters, 101 finishers

Rear-engined dominance by Porsche

Praise be – a Monte Carlo rally without handicaps, performance factors, or weird limitations on cars or their equipment! Had sanity finally crept into the event?

In 1968, at last, it looked like that. As I wrote in *Autocar* in January 1968:

'What was, frankly, a few years ago a rally ruled by the whims of the organisers (who set handicaps and indices of performance to suit themselves), has now developed into a thoroughly sporting winter race ...'

– and so it had. For the first time in many years the serious 'works' teams (for the time was long past when a private owner stood a chance of success) could plan logically, on the basis of cars, drivers and – most important of all – tyres.

Since 1967 the balance of power had changed, significantly. The front-wheel-drive Minis had run out of development potential, while rear-engined cars like the lightweight Alpine-Renaults and the Porsche 911s were improving all the time. Both had won major events in 1967, and the combination of Vic Elford in a 911 was now the standard which others had to beat. Lancia's Fulvia HFs were getting better all the time.

For 1968 there was the usual plethora of starting points, all quite equally patronised, and the total entry was 229 cars, as in 1967. The shambles of 1966 seemed to have been forgotten. Thirty-one British crews chose to start from Dover, where they actually moved off from a parking area at the port, straight on to the cross-channel ferry to Boulogne, which left at 02.30 hrs. in the morning. There were no special stages before the arrival in Monte Carlo. As usual there was a *Parcours Commun*, of 930 miles, this time with seven stages, the longest being 46 km. from La Madeleine, via Barcillonette, to Gap. The first was a 25 km. section from Pont des Miolans to St. Auban, more familiar in Alpine rallies held in high summer, the shortest being a final 10 km. blast up Levens, just before the finish.

From the eight starting points the run down to Monte Carlo was easy, and most of the 153 surviving crews were complaining of boredom when they arrived; almost all of them were unpenalised. What followed, in the next two sessions, was really a winter motor race, for there was little snow, and most stages were dry and clear.

Right from the start, on the *Parcours Commun*, it was clear that the days of BMC domination were over. In spite of having even more powerful engines than usual (with special single-choke versions of the famous twin-choke Weber carburettor), they were well off the pace. In seven stages, the quickest driver (Rauno Aaltonen) lost 117 seconds to the leading rear-engined cars, and only Timo Makinen (once) set a 'top three' stage time.

Up front, the Lancias were as fast as the Minis, but the battle for the lead was between Porsche (Vic Elford and Pauli Toivonen), and Alpine-Renault (Guy Larrousse, Jean-Francis Piot, Jean-Claude Andruet and Jean Vinatier). By the end of the loop Piot and Andruet had both disappeared – one with a broken distributor, the other well off the road. Makinen's Mini-Cooper S blew its engine, though Paddy Hopkirk and Tony Fall were still in contention.

When 83 cars arrived back in Monte Carlo, only 25 had not been penalised on a very tight road section. Vic Elford was complaining that one of his stage times was wrong by a full minute, and the result was that he lay second, just 14 seconds behind Gerard Larrousse's Alpine-Renault, and 49 seconds ahead of Pauli Toivonen's Porsche 911. Three minutes covered the top five cars. In the top ten, five cars had rear engines and rear-drive, the other five having front engines and front-drive – the trends

were obvious!

On the Thursday night, 60 crews faced the usual flat out race round the Mountain circuit which, as ever, included six special stages, three of which were 'up and over' assaults of the Col du Turini, two being the very fast Col de Couillole from St. Sauveur to Beuil; every 'works' team now used ice-notes crews, and a straight speed contest was in prospect. The only real snow was at the top of the Turini.

Elford's Porsche was invincible (BMC team manager Peter Browning called this 'a chilly Alpine') and outpaced Toivonen's sister car. Larrousse's Alpine-Renault, however, *could* still have won if it had not crashed on fresh snow on the second passage of the Turini. Unconfirmed stories were that this snow had been shovelled into the road by drunken spectators – but by Frenchmen, to trip up a French car? Surely not?

Porsche, therefore, finished first and second, though BMC's 'works' Minis finished with honour, in third, fourth and fifth places. BMC and Lancia won the main team prizes, while Pat Moss-Carlsson (Lancia Fulvia HF) won the Ladies' Prize. Except for Alpine-Renault, almost everyone had something to boast about.

1968

The first 'no-handicap/performance-factor' event for many years: starting points from Athens, Dover, Frankfurt, Lisbon, Monte Carlo, Oslo, Rheims, Warsaw: common route from arrival in Monte Carlo.

    1. V. Elford – D. Stone   (Porsche 911T) Warsaw
2. P. Toivonen – M. Tiukkanen   (Porsche 911S)
    3. R. Aaltonen – H. Liddon   (BMC Mini-Cooper S)
      4. A. Fall – M. Wood   (BMC Mini-Cooper S)
     5. P. Hopkirk – R. Crellin   (BMC Mini-Cooper S)
6. O. Andersson – J. Davenport   (Lancia Fulvia HF)

229 entries, 200 starters, 153 reached Monte Carlo

Porsche's repeat performance

In the two previous years Vic Elford had shown just how good the rear-engined Porsche could be on the Monte Carlo rally. Now in 1969, a brave young Swede called Bjorn Waldegard repeated the demonstration. The Mini era was now past, and it was time for the rear-engined cars to make all the headlines.

Once again the total entry had sagged a little. The profile of the entry, too, was progressively changing – there were fewer true 'amateur' entries, and few publicity-seekers by this time, and even the private owners tried to do as serious and professional job as they could.

The organisers, in any case, had now washed their hands of handicaps, there were no post-rally diversions, while the route and the stages were now tailored to the liking of the 'works' teams. The real rally started from Monte Carlo after competitors had trekked across Europe for the first 48 hours.

Could it be improved even further? Certainly, for according to the professionals, all that was now needed was for the long concentration runs to be abandoned altogether.

But that was not likely to happen. As in the past, the organisers provided a choice of starting points, as glamorous as Athens, or as seedily ordinary as London Heathrow Airport. Five of the routes met at Perigueux (east of Bordeaux), seven took the same route from St. Claude to Monte Carlo, while the small Athens contingent did their own trekking all the way through Greece, Yugoslavia and northern Italy.

As a Monte Carlo rally starting point, Great Britain was fast losing its charm. On this occasion only 23 crews chose the London start point, with Ove Andersson's Escort Twin Cam and Pat Moss-Carlsson's Lancia Fulvia HF leading the column. Andersson left Heathrow at 18.45 hrs. on Friday, January 17th, then travelled by way of Dover, Boulogne, Brussels, Ostend, Rennes and Perigueux.

The long Common Route, to be tackled by all crews, was a long and gruelling loop – 950 miles from Monte Carlo to Monte Carlo, going as far west as the Burzet stages, as far north as Chambery, and taking in eight long special stages on the way. Some stages, like Pont des Miolans to St. Auban, the St. Jean circuit, and the Col du Granier (north to south, this time) were familiar, but others like the Burzet loop were still relatively new hazards.

Everyone agreed that it would not feel the same without a team of BMC Mini-Coopers, but that 'works' effort had now been abandoned in favour of an assault on circuit racing and rallycross. Ford, however, sent three Escort Twin-Cams, Lancia sent a fleet of Fulvia HFs, there were four Porsche 911Ss, several Alpine-Renaults, Citroën DS21s, a BMW 2002 Ti for Timo Makinen, a Saab Sonett V4 for Simo Lampinen, and other well-fancied private owners.

During the 1960s, studded tyre technology had advanced to such an extent that most private owners could afford to buy the best, and the run to Monte Carlo had long since ceased to be a stopper. Even so, conditions were such that only 111 of the 158 arrivals still had a clean sheet. Twenty-five crews had already retired. Most of the ice and snow had been found in the *Massif Central*, which the luckless Monte Carlo starters had had to tackle twice. From Athens, though, the roads were almost completely clear.

Common Route conditions were perfect for the Porsches and the Alpine-Renaults, for they had lots of traction where there was ice and snow, and loads of performance where the roads were clear. Bjorn Waldegard (Porsche 911S) vied with his team mates and rivals Vic Elford and Pauli Toivonen for the lead while the rest of the field began to eliminate itself. Rauno Aaltonen and Tony Fall both crashed their Lancias on the same stretch of road, Timo Makinen's BMW ran out of rear brakes, while Ove Andersson's Escort Twin-Cam broke its transmission, and

Hannu Mikkola crashed his Escort and deranged the front suspension.

It was an enormously demanding loop, which eliminated many crews. One-hundred-and-fifty-eight cars had started, but only 39 cars finished it. There was no doubt that Porsche 911s were in command, for at this point Waldegard's car led Vic Elford's car by 89 seconds. Jean Vinatier, in the best of the Alpine-Renaults, was third, 4 min. 31 sec. off the pace, with Gerard Larrousse's Porsche 911 not far behind.

On the Thursday night all 39 surviving crews tackled the 420 mile Mountain Circuit, a complex route very similar to that used in 1968. There were seven special stages – with the Col du Turini tackled three times (once westbound, twice eastbound) – and literally nowhere to take a breather.

As the night began, Elford overhauled Waldegard, and began to increase his lead then, after the fourth stage, and close to his service crew at Sospel, he went off the road, hit a tree, and ended his rally there and then. Larrousse passed Vinatier during the night, and Jean-Francois Piot did well to put his 'works' Escort Twin-Cam into fourth place.

Only 27 cars made it to the end. It had been a real winter race.

1969

Starting points from Athens, Frankfurt, Lisbon, London, Monte Carlo, Oslo, Rheims, Warsaw: common route from arrival in Monte Carlo.

1. *B. Waldegard – B. Helmer*   (*Porsche 911*) *Warsaw*
2. *G. Larrousse –*
   J. C. Perramond   (*Porsche 911*)
3. *J. Vinatier – J-F. Jacob*   (*Alpine-Renault A110*)
4. *J-F. Piot – J. Todt*   (*Ford Escort TC*)
5. *J-L. Therier – M. Callewaert*   (*Renault R8 Gordini*)
6. *Ms. P. Moss-Carlsson –*
   Ms. E. Nystrom   (*Lancia Fulvia HF*)

212 entries, 183 starters, 158 reached Monte Carlo, 39 finished Common Route, 27 finishers

Porsche versus Alpine-Renault, as before

If you had gone to sleep immediately after the end of the 1969 rally, then been awakened at the start of the 1970 event, you would have noticed few differences. The routes were almost the same, the stages were almost the same – and the cars all seemed to be the same. On this, as on several other Monte Carlo rally occasions, it was a return fight.

The organisers, clearly, were very happy with the 'plot' which they had established in previous years. Except that the London start had been abandoned, with cars starting from a garage in Dover and driving straight on to the ferry which was to take them to Boulogne, British starters were faced with a similar run to the Mediterranean as in 1969. There was variation on a theme, through Czechoslovakia, Austria and West Germany, for the Oslo and Warsaw starters, while Athens runners joined the other seven start points at Gap for a final blast over the Alps to Monte Carlo.

In spite of the carnage of 1969 – only 27 finishers from 183 starters – the entry held up remarkably well once again. In the UK, exchange control regulations had been eased, which should have made it easier to encourage British entries; even so, the use of Dover was a complete flop, with only eight cars electing to start from there. There were, indeed, only 13 British

private entries – a far cry from the mid-1950s when more than 400 drivers had regularly fought for a place in the event.

The 'works' entry was small, but select, and as the entry was now properly 'seeded' it was certain that the winner would come from one of the first 20 runners. Three works Porsches faced up to five Alpine-Renaults, six Lancia Fulvia HFs, and three Ford Escort Twin-Cams, with a single Saab V4 to add spice.

The big change, here, was that Stuart Turner, after two years out of motor sport, had taken control at Ford; for 1970 the 'works' Twin-Cams were as close to being 'ice-racers' as could be arranged.

Once again, as so often in post-war years, the rally was let down by the weather, for there was cold but essentially clear and dry weather from all eight starting points. No fewer than 157 of the 184 starters reached Monte Carlo. Since the weather forecast for the Common Route was 'good, with little chance of snow', this looked like being another Porsche benefit.

And so it proved. The nine special stages in the long, 26-hour, loop were totally dominated by Porsche, where most of the roads were dry, and retirements generally came from the cars being overworked, rather than them sliding off the road when fighting for grip.

Even so, the 'works' contingent was soon depleted – for Tony Fall's Lancia blew its engine on the first stage and Jean Vinatier's Alpine-Renault ruined its racing tyre treads. Later Hannu Mikkola's Escort Twin-Cam jammed its gearbox, which did nothing for the Boreham team's chances.

In nine stages Bjorn Waldegard's Porsche 911S had pulled out 1 min. 52 sec. on J-P. Nicolas's Alpine-Renault, with two other Porsches behind him, and with three Lancias and three Escorts filling up the top ten at that stage. Porsche 911Ss had been fastest on six stages, with an Alpine Renault, an Escort and a Lancia fastest on one stage each. Roger Clark, who was driving his heart out on a rally favouring the rear-engined machines, was down in sixth place.

The Mountain Circuit, though not quite as snow free as the earlier loop, was still remarkably clear when the top sixty crews set out for an 11-hour blast around the mountains. As in 1969 there were seven special stages, with the Turini tackled three times, and the Cols de Couillole and Madone twice each. One measure of the weather was that only seven kilometres of the 23 km. Turini had any snow cover.

It was another crushing demonstration of Porsche strength, performance and durability, for one or other of the orange cars was fastest on six of the seven stages. To rub it in, one of the Porsches was second fastest on another six occasions too.

There was nothing that any other competitor could do, and in the end 'Jumbo' Nicolas's Alpine had to settle for third place. Roger Clark drove the rally of his career, so far, but could not do any better than fifth place, while Timo Makinen (also in an Escort Twin-Cam) recovered ground to take seventh place.

Could nothing stop the Porsche juggernaut? Ford went away to plan a mid-engined special (the GT70 project, which came to nothing), while Alpine-Renault returned to Paris, determined to do even better in 1971.

1970

Starting points from Athens, Dover, Frankfurt, Lisbon, Monte Carlo, Oslo, Rheims, Warsaw: common route from arrival in Monte Carlo.

  1. *B. Waldegard – L. Helmer* *(Porsche 911S) Oslo*
  2. *G. Larrousse – M. Gelin* *(Porsche 911S)*
  3. *J-P. Nicolas – C. Roure* *(Alpine-Renault A110)*
  4. *A. Andersson – B. Thorszelius* *(Porsche 911)*
  5. *R. Clark – J. Porter* *(Ford Escort TC)*
  6. *A. Ballestrieri – D. Audetto* *(Lancia Fulvia HF)*

232 entries, 184 starters, 157 reached Monte Carlo, 77 finishers

Alpine-Renault, decisively

When Alpine-Renault took first, second and third places in the 1971 rally, there was a huge and collective sigh of relief throughout the French motor sporting media. The rear-engined Alpines had been so fast, so promising, but so unlucky, for such a long time that it began to look as if the French snows had a jinx on them.

Even in 1971, though, there were special circumstances. Porsche, for marketing reasons bitterly resented by the drivers, chose to use the new mid-engined 914/6 models instead of the ferociously effective rear-engined 911s. It was a strategy which misfired completely – the new car was not as wieldy on snow and ice as its elder relative, and not even Bjorn Waldegard could stay on terms with the tiny French coupés.

The rally organisers did not rest on their laurels, even though they were well pleased with the results in previous years. There were new starting points and new routes, one special stage on the way down from Gap to Monte Carlo, and the usual two long loops – the Common Route and the Mountain Circuit – to be tackled after arrival.

On this occasion there was a re-shuffle of starting points and routes to the Mediterranean. Compared with 1970, Lisbon and Dover were abandoned.

Glasgow, last used in 1964, was reinstated, Bucharest came back after a very long absence indeed, there was a Spanish start from Almeria but – most enterprising of all – there was also to be a start from Marrakech, in Morocco.

Marrakech proved remarkably popular, with 38 electing to start from there – not merely because it was a nice place to visit in a European winter, but because the route crossed the Straits of Gibralter at Algeciras, and hugged the Mediterranean shore all the way to Narbonne, before striking inland for the final meeting point at Gap. The choice of Glasgow, however, was a miserable failure, for only ten crews (all British) chose it. Since they left Blythswood Square at 8 p.m. on Friday, January 22nd, drove through the night via Scotch Corner and Rugby, and left Dover at 10 a.m. the following day, few people even knew there *was* a Monte Carlo rally in Britain in 1971.

For the first time since the 1950s there were no British 'works' cars in the 254-strong entry list, for BMC was out of rallying, and Ford knew it could not win the event without a new design of car. The main battle, for sure, was going to between the *seven* (and that's no misprint) Alpine-Renaults, the five Lancia Fulvia HFs, three new Datsun 240Zs, four Porsche

Photo on p. 136
Lancia developed the front-drive Fulvia HF over several years, eventually winning in 1972. In 1971 this 1.6-litre example was driven by Sergio Barbasio, who started from Marrakech.

Top photo, p. 137
In 1971 The Scotsman newspaper sponsored this Group 1 Mini-Cooper S entry for Andrew Cowan and Johnstone Syer, who started from Glasgow and finished 21st.

Bottom photo, p. 137
This was one of five Lancia Fulvia 1600HF cars to be entered in 1971 – the best of which finished sixth, behind three Alpine-Renaults, a Porsche 914/6 and a Datsun 240Z.

Photo above
For a time in the late 1960s/early 1970s the 1.9-litre Opel Kadett GT/E was a competitive Group 1 car, especially if the Monte weather was spring-like, as seen here in 1971.

914/6s, several BMWs, and two Fiats – the 'pecking order' of factory teams was changing, for Fiat was newly-founded, and Datsun was testing the water in Europe for the first time.

As so often in recent years, there was virtually no snow to be faced before all ten columns got together at Gap. The first 'sorting out' special stage – a 38 km. affair from Rouaine to Pont des Miolans (south of the Entrevaux-Puget Theniers main road), had been a novelty in the summer Alpine rally only a few years earlier.

Except that the entry was still not seeded at this point – which meant that the 'works' Lancias tackled it five *hours* after the early runners from Marrakech – this twisty horror, 60 per cent covered with hard rutted ice, was a demanding test. Ove Andersson's Alpine-Renault was fastest from his team mate Jean-Luc Therier, and Sandro Munari's Lancia. One-hundred-and-seventy-one crews reached Monte Carlo.

The long (940 mile) Common Route, which started on the Tuesday morning, included nine speed tests totalling 151 miles, and was very similar to that used in 1969 and 1970, as it stretched east to

Burzet, north to Chambery, and passed through Gap and Digne on the way back to Monte Carlo.

Although conditions on each of the nine stages varied considerably – from snow storms in the Burzet loop to dry tarmac at Le Moulinon and up La Rochette – and no fewer than five drivers set a fastest time, Ove Andersson and David Stone led all the way, in their 155 b.h.p., 1.6 litre, Alpine-Renault. Seventeen seconds ahead of Therier at the start, they increased this to 31 seconds (over J-C. Andruet), while Therier slipped to third. Waldegard's twitchy-handling Porsche was fourth, 66 seconds behind, and the rest were struggling.

The Common Route had decimated the field, for only 30 cars returned to Monte Carlo. Even so, with a seven-stage Mountain Circuit (the same as in previous years) to come, the outcome was still not settled – or so Porsche and Lancia hoped . . .

Nothing, in fact, was changed by the final (Thursday) night, except that Therier pushed past Andruet to take second place behind Ove Andersson. The genial Swede took two fastest times, but Waldegard only one – the result being a win by 40 seconds, but by 111 seconds from the Porsche.

1971

Starting points from Almeria, Athens, Bucharest, Frankfurt, Glasgow, Marrakech, Monte Carlo, Oslo, Rheims, Warsaw: common route from Gap.

1.	O. Andersson – D. Stone	(Alpine-Renault A110)	Marrakech
2.	J-L. Therier – M. Callewaert	(Alpine-Renault A110)	
3.	J-C. Andruet – G. Vial	(Alpine-Renault A110)	
4.	B. Waldegard – H. Thorszelius	(Porsche 914/6)	
5.	R. Aaltonen – P. Easter	(Datsun 240Z)	
6.	S. Lampinen – J. Davenport	(Lancia Fulvia HF)	

254 entries, 248 starters, 171 reached Monte Carlo, 30 finished Common Route, 22 finishers

1972

Lancia's surprise victory

There had been so many novelties in the 1971 event, along with a popular victory for Alpine-Renault, that the entry for the 1972 rally was well up on previous years. Two-hundred-and-ninety-nine crews paid their money (though only 264 of them started) – a figure not seen since 1964. Perhaps it wasn't surprising to see 29 Alpine-Renaults in the list.

Once more there were changes to the format. After only one year the Moroccan start, at Marrakech, was abandoned, and as the organisers had also decided to scrub out the 'classification' stage over the Col de Perty on the run down to Monte Carlo (at a very late stage in planning) the choice of starting points was no longer critical.

In the end 56 crews elected to start from sunny Almeria, in southern Spain, mainly because the authorities offered free accommodation at the start. There were 44 from Warsaw and Frankfurt, and 41 each from Athens and Monte Carlo itself. Lisbon came back and Glasgow was retained, but one wonders why – only eight and nine crews, respectively, chose these places.

Although the event's character had not changed, there were different cars and teams present. As in 1971 Alpine-Renault and Lancia were out in force. Fiat's effort (in 124 Spiders) was growing all the

time, Porsche had no 'works' cars, but Shell-France sponsored two 911S models for Bjorn Waldegard and Gerard Larrousse, Datsun entered two 240Z Coupés, while Ford came back seriously, with Escort RS1600s for Timo Makinen, and Jean-François Piot.

The various runs to Monte Carlo were completed in mild weather. Even though the classification stage had been called, there was still a very nasty 76 km. road section to be completed at high speed; this penalised no fewer than 122 crews, including Piot's works Escort RS1600. Even so, 244 crews reached Monte Carlo, with a night's sleep ahead of them before they tackled the well-known eight-stage, 26-hour Common Route.

The big change in the Common Route was the abandoning of the 6 km. Levens stage, in favour of the 328 km. Rouaine-Pont des Miolans stage (which had been used for the first time in the 1971 concentration runs). One-hundred-and-ninety-seven cars left Monte Carlo to start this test, but only 33 of them were destined to complete it.

In 26 hours the drivers had to face every possible combination of 'Monte Carlo' weather – dry stages requiring racing tyres near the start and finish, blizzard conditions in the Ardeche at Burzet, and a mixture further north. The 'works' teams, with their enormous tyre stocks, could cope, but the private owners were soon in dreadful trouble. The road sections were so tight in places that most crews – private or factory-entered – were penalised.

It was not an event which developed according to the form-book. On the eight stages of the Common Route and the seven stages of the Mountain Circuit, Sandro Munari's 1.6 litre Lancia Fulvia HF set only one fastest time, yet at the end of the day he won the rally by no less than 11 *minutes*!

On the Common Route Alpine-Renault reinforced their 1971 performance, and after the 26-hour thrash around the mountains its cars held first, second, fourth and sixth places; Ove Andersson was just three seconds ahead of Bernard Darniche, with Munari's Lancia a mere 10 seconds off the pace. Bjorn Waldegard's Porsche 911S had set three fastest times, but went off the road on the last (Rouaine) stage, losing more than an hour! Ford's Escort RS1600s were struggling for grip, down in eighth and ninth places, and *20 minutes* adrift.

The seven-stage, 12-hour Mountain Circuit, the same challenge as in the last few years, with only three stretches of road timed to the second (the Turini used three times) but *every* road section very tight indeed, was set to be a titanic shoot-out between Alpine-Renault and Lancia, especially as road conditions were quite variable, with a lot of fresh snow on the Turini.

Except that Alpine-Renault blew it. Although Bernard Darniche set three fastest times (and Larrousse's Porsche two fastest times), not one of the four leading cars finished the night – Ove Andersson's and Darniche's cars broke their gearboxes, Andruet crashed after a brake failure, and finally J-P. Nicolas also crashed his car. Within an hour the hopes of the French had completely evaporated.

'On the night' Gerard Larrousse's Porsche was fastest of all, his performance bringing him back up to second place (he was getting used to finishing second – that made it three times, 1969, 1970 and now 1972 . . .), though Rauno Aaltonen also stormed up from seventh to second. The imperturbable Munari, however, settled for a string of second and third fastest times, yet still strolled off with the victory.

The Lancia team was ecstatic – was this the start of Italian dominance in the 1970s?

1972

Starting points from Almeria, Athens, Frankfurt, Glasgow, Lisbon, Monte Carlo, Oslo, Rheims, Warsaw: common route from arrival in Monte Carlo

1.	S. Munari – M. Mannucci	(Lancia Fulvia HF) Almeria
2.	G. Larrousse	
	J-C. Perramond	(Porsche 911S)
3.	R. Aaltonen – J. Todt	(Datsun 240Z)
4.	S. Lampinen – S. Andreasson	(Lancis Fulvia HF)
5.	J-F. Piot – J. Porter	(Ford Escort RS1600)
6.	S. Barbasio – P. Sodano	(Lancia Fulvia HF)

299 entries, 266 starters, 244 reached Monte Carlo, 33 finished Common Route, 24 finishers

A shambles!

Although the results of the event show an event dominated by Alpine-Renault, competitors and historians recall the rally, simply, as a disgraceful shambles. The organisers completely lost control, treated competitors disgracefully, and almost had full-scale riots on their hands. It was the first (and, so far, only) time that a rally has *almost* been brought to a halt by competitor power.

Events came to a head on the Burzet loop, half-way round the Common Route, when crashed cars on the special stage caused a wholesale blockage. One-hundred-and-forty-four cars were denied a chance to tackle the stage. The organisers then arrogantly stated that they had to be disqualified, and the surviving 65 cars carried on.

Incensed by this, the disqualified crews made off across country to Digne, blocked the rally route and prepared for a pitched battle. Some competitors, officially still in the running, had to find other routes, some charged round the blockages, and some offered violence.

It was a shambles, for which the organisers offered no more than shoulder-shrugging and bland expressions. Even though disqualified crews were offered free entries for 1974, the event should have died, there and then. Perhaps, if the Energy Crisis

had not intervened and made sure the 1974 event was cancelled, it might have done so...

Even before the trouble erupted, there was controversy, though the event looked to be even more popular than ever. No fewer than 322 crews entered, a further increase on 1972 – and this in spite of an early proposal to ban studs on the only special stage (Le Col du Corobin) scheduled to take place on the concentration run from Digne to Monte Carlo. That proposal was abandoned when the factory teams *and* the tyre companies protested.

Factory interest was as high as ever, for Alpine-Renault's five-car fleet of 1.8 litre cars was matched by three Lancia Fulvia HFs, four Fiat 124 Abarth Spiders, two Datsun 240Zs, and two Ford Escort RS1600s with newly-developed 2 litre alloy-blocked engines. Surprisingly, there were no competitive Porsches.

Once again the starting points had been re-shuffled, with Rome making a re-appearance, and Lisbon dropping out again. The organisers persisted in the use of Glasgow, but only 14 crews chose it. The meat of the rally was the same as usual – with the Common Route to and from Burzet, followed by the Mountain Circuit for the top 60 crews.

After the Corobin test, Ford was delighted to see

Hannu Mikkola sharing fastest time with Sandro Munari's Lancia, with Timo Makinen in third place. It was tyre choice, rather than car superiority, which brought this about, for the Alpine-Renaults were well back even though they were expected to take the lead on the Common Route. The majority of cars had been booked for speeding by the ruthless French police – and the Corobin test had run two hours behind schedule . . .

One day before the 1,040-mile, 31 hr. Common Route started, three of the 10 scheduled stages were blocked by snow which, among other things, made the task of the factory 'ice-notes' crews quite impossible. There was a lot of snow everywhere, which made the Alpine-Renault team even more confident.

As expected the Alpine-Renaults dominated proceedings, with all the team cars storming up the order; compared with 1972, the cars were not only faster, with larger engines and more torque, but much more reliable too. Surprisingly, only the two 'works' Escort RS1600s could hold on to this pace, with Mikkola and Makinen both setting stunning stage times.

The contest, as such, really fizzled out on the Burzet loop, for only 65 cars recorded times before it became completely blocked. Before the survivors came back to Monte Carlo (that process, incidentally, including a complete cancellation of two stages on the original route after Seyne-les-Alpes after the blockage was set up) three of the Lancias had disappeared, including the 1972 victor, Sandro Munari, who had gone off the road.

By the time the Mountain Circuit began on the Thursday evening, Alpine-Renault was expected to win – but, then, French enthusiasts remembered the disasters of 1972, and crossed their fingers. In the event, it was Makinen's Escort which had the disaster, for it lost a front wheel on the Turini and lost five minutes while the spare was being fitted. Six different people set fastest stage times (including, remarkably, two fastest times for Makinen's Escort), and because Alpine-Renault fought against Alpine-Renault the result was close. In the end Andruet's car beat Ove Andersson's car by a mere 26 sec. – and there were five Alpine-Renaults in the top six.

Starting points from Almeria, Athens, Frankfurt, Glasgow, Monte Carlo, Oslo, Rheims, Rome and Warsaw: common route from Ales

    C. Andruet – 'Biche'   (Alpine-Renault A110)
2. O. Andersson – J. Todt   (Alpine-Renault A110)
3. J-P. Nicolas – M. Vial   (Alpine-Renault A110)
4. H. Mikkola – J. Porter   (Ford Escort RS1600)
5. J-L. Therier – M. Callewaert   (Alpine-Renault A110)
6. J-F. Piot – J-L. Marnat   (Alpine-Renault A110)

322 entries, 278 starters, 51 qualified finishers, 44 finished all route

Crushing victory for Lancia's Stratos

1974 — a re-run of 1957

Just as the 1957 rally had been sunk by a Middle East war in 1956, so was the 1974 event scuppered by a Middle East war in 1973. Seventeen years on, it was a complete re-run. The Israelis battled with the Arabs in a war which was brief and bloody, and one result was a disruption of oil supplies. This time round, the extra complications were Arab embargos on the supply of oil to certain countries, and a huge increase in the price of that oil which *was* made available.

This time, though, it never looked likely that the event would be held, for the fuel supply problem, allied to what became known as the Energy Crisis, was very serious indeed. As in 1957, however, things improved rapidly in 1974 and, although petrol soon became much more expensive than it had been a year earlier, there was no danger that the 1975 rally would also be cancelled.

Even though it was two years since the chaotic series of events surrounding the 1973 rally, Europe's competitors had not forgiven the organisers of the Monte Carlo rally. When the event was re-born, after its enforced layoff in 1974, a mere 96 crews decided to enter. This was a far cry from the great days of the event, in the 1950s and early 1960s – but no-one seemed to be sympathetic...

The statistics tell their own story – 96 starters, 43 finished the Common Route, and only 30 completed the Mountain Circuit. This was the lowest turn-out for almost 50 years. Not only that, but the battle for outright victory was joined by only four factory teams – Lancia, Renault, Fiat and Opel. In any case, the organisers had also reneged on their offer of a free entry to those disqualified in 1973 – they deserved nothing better.

Lancia turned up with three of the magnificent new mid-engined Stratos coupés, which had only recently been homologated but which were already *the* cars to beat in all circumstances. Renault entered a brace of the new (and larger) Type 310s, but there were two of the traditional Type 110 Berlinettes for J-P. Nicolas and Jean Ragnotti to drive. Fiat's four 16-valve 124 Spider Abarths were driven by stars like Hannu Mikkola, Markku Alen and Bernard

Lancia's sensational mid-engined Stratos was probably the most effective two-wheel-drive car ever to tackle the Monte. In 1975 Sandro Munari and Mario Mannucci won the event at a canter from the Fiat Abarth team – the first of three consecutive victories.

Darniche, while Opel were using two relatively unknowns – Anders Kullang and a lanky West German called Walter Rohrl. The world of rallying was to hear much more about him in the next few years!

In spite of the ignominy of 1973, the organisers still seemed to lack commonsense. One might think that the time had come to drop a British start because it was unpopular. Not so – instead, an Aberdeen start point was proposed, with intermediate controls at Stranraer, in Carmathen and at Land's End on the way to Dover! Not unnaturally, no-one chose to use this route – the two British entrants (Tony Maslen and Doug Harris in Escorts) electing to start from Monte Carlo instead.

On this occasion there were only five starting points, of which Agadir in Morocco sounded much the most glamorous. This route didn't involve snow, but started with a dust storm before Marrakech. There were some extremely odd routings – Monte Carlo starters went down through Italy to Naples, then doubled back to Cortina, before returning to Gap; Agadir starters went via Lisbon, while Stockholm and Warsaw crews also joined the Monte Carlo and Athens runners at Cortina.

A series of tired and bored crews, 86 out of the original 96, arrived in Gap on the Saturday morning, after which they faced four special stages on the way to Monte Carlo, two in France and two close to San Remo, in Italy. There was snow on the opening stage, but rain, mud and rocks on the other three.

Lancia had already lost Ballestrieri's Beta Coupé soon after the start, with a blown engine. Then, on the second stage, both Andruet and Pinto crashed their Stratoses at the same place, on a corner marked as 'wet' by the ice-note crews, but which had frozen over in the meantime. Munari's car didn't crash – quite – but from that point he was fighting a lone battle against the rest of the field.

Surprisingly the Alpine-Renaults were never in contention, so for the rest of the event the fight was between one Lancia, four Fiats and Walter Rohrl's Opel Ascona. When the rally reached Monte Carlo on the Sunday, the Stratos already led by 1 min. 55 sec. from three Fiats.

Compared with 1973, the Common Route had been slightly shortened, as had the length of the special stages. Not that this made the slightest difference to Lancia, since Munari's Stratos pulled gradually and inexorably away from the rest of the field. As the Lancia was running first on the road, it could always get the best and latest information about tyres; team chief Cesare Fiorio kept a very careful eye on the Fiats, and ran a very controlled campaign.

On the nine special stages Munari's Stratos was fastest only twice, but second fastest four times. Hannu Mikkola and Markku Alen had a monumental scrap in their Fiat 124 Abarth Spiders, while J-P. Nicolas's old-style Alpine-Renault challenge held up well until he crashed on the eighth stage. Team-mates Ragnotti and Therier had already done the same.

After another night's sleep the Lancia set out on the famous Mountain Circuit to defend a lead of 3 min. 22 sec., which looked quite secure. Only 42 other cars joined him, on a route where plenty of fresh snow had been shovelled down off the banks by boisterous spectators.

Just to rub it in, Munari set four fastest times, though Hannu Mikkola (three times) and Markku Alen (twice) kept him awake. At the end of a very predictable event the Stratos was 3 min. 6 sec. in the clear, though Mikkola only beat his team mate by 41 sec.

1975

Starting points from Agadir, Athens, Monte Carlo, Stockholm and Warsaw: common route from Gap.

1. S. Munari – M. Mannucci   (*Lancia Stratos*)
2. H. Mikkola – J. Todt   (*Fiat Abarth 124 Rallye*)
3. M. Alen – I. Kivimaki   (*Fiat Abarth 124 Rallye*)
4. F. Bacchelli – B. Scabini   (*Fiat Abarth 124 Rallye*)
5. J-F. Piot – J. de Alexandris   (*Renault 17 Gordini*)
6. J. Henry – M. Gelin   (*Alpine-Renault A110*)

96 starters, 43 qualified as finishers, 30 completed route

No competition for the Stratos

Somehow, over the years, the Monte organisers earned something of an unfortunate reputation – they could never leave well alone. After several years of stability, in which the rally had become a genuine 'winter race' with the fastest car-driver combination winning, they chose to alter the format for 1976.

It was all incredibly misguided. By insisting that all entrants specified the type of tyres they would use *a full week before the event started*, the organisers hoped to strike a blow against the excesses of the factory teams and give the private owners an even chance.

It was a stupid strateg*y*, which completely misfired. Although every crew had its tyre treads recorded by the organisers (by driving the car over sheets of paper to have imprints etched on them), there was no limitation on compounds, or on the number, type, and pattern of studding to be used. The fact that private owners neither had the cars nor the driving skills to challenge the 'works' drivers was one factor – their sheer financial inability to cope with these rules was the clincher.

On the other hand, the organisers balanced this lunacy with a simplification of the routes. Although there were still seven starting points, all routes led more or less directly to Monte Carlo, virtually halving the run in from the 4,000 km. of 1975 to around 2,000 km. in 1976. The routes did not join up before Monte Carlo was reached, after which two stages (49 km. in all) were tackled in Italy, above San Remo, before the crews then had their night's rest.

After this there was the usual long and demanding 36-hour *Parcours Commun* to be tackled by all surviving crews – this taking in 12 stages and including short halts at Gap and Vals les Bains. Then, after another night's sleep, came the final flat-out dash around the Mountain Circuit, taking in nine stages, *each one* of which was tackled three times! That, at least, made the practising and the pace notes easier to organise!

Since 1975 the mid-engined Lancia Stratos had become virtually unbeatable in world-class rallying, so no-one truthfully expected to be ahead of a Stratos at the end of this event. Lancia entered four cars – one of them being entered by the French Lancia importer, and driven by Bernard Darniche – but the battle for victory looked sure to be between Munari and Bjorn Waldegard. Ford entered two tarmac-spec. Escort RS1800s for Timo Makinen and Roger Clark, Fiat had three fuel-injected 16-valve 124 Abarth Spiders, Opel had three 2 litre Kadetts, while Alpine-Renault hired out several 'works' A310s to

Top photo, p. 148
Pre-start concentration for the celebrated British crew of Roger Clark (at the wheel) and Jim Porter, before beginning the 1976 event in their 'works' Ford Escort RS1800. They finished fifth overall.

Bottom photo, p. 148
Mid-1970s tyre technology included carefully-profiled tyre treads in which the blocks could 'work' to clear out the snow, and in which pin studs could be fitted to give maximum traction.

Photo above
Roger Clark-Jim Porter (Ford Escort RS1800) ready to start the 1976 event from London, the car well-plastered with sponsorship stickers from Shell and Dunlop. The reward was fifth, well behind Munari's winning Lancia Stratos.

drivers like J-P. Nicolas, J-C. Andruet and J-C. Therier.

The total entry, at least, had recovered somewhat from the humiliations of 1975; even so, only 148 crews faced the starting flag. The British entry was pathetically small, and the London start was almost deserted, even though Minister for Sport Dennis Howell was on hand to drop the flag. The weather was amazingly mild, and there was no snow, and only a hint of ice on the two Italian stages, which were tackled at night. Right away, Sandro Munari put his Stratos into the lead, from Andruet's Alpine-Renault; Bjorn Waldegard and Raffaele Pinto (also in Stratos cars) were not far behind.

On the *Parcours Commun* the Lancia team sorted out its troops, and began to show off the invincibility of the Stratos. On almost every special stage, whether it was day or night, short or long, clear or icy, Munari or Waldegard set the fastest times. Later it became clear that the blonde Swede was driving to orders. Lancia team boss Cesare Fiorio wanted Munari to win, so that he could claim his hat-trick of successes (1972, 1975 and 1976), and Waldegard was expected to finish a close, but loyally subordinate, second.

In the meantime Pinto's Stratos broke its engine, Mikkola's Opel Kadett broke its gearbox, and Kullang's Kadett its engine. Both Escorts went well in spite of handling problems, then Makinen's car blew a head gasket and had to retire. Two of the three Fiats retired with engine problems, while Markku Alen's car recovered from a poor start.

It was another of those unfortunate events where the Alpine-Renault attack evaporated completely. Nicolas's car broke its transmission on the last night when in fourth place, Andruet crashed his car on a road section (when he was in third place behind the Lancias), Therier crashed his car too, while Marie-Claude Beaumont's car suffered fuel pump failure at the worst possible moment.

Even before the last night the positions had settled down – three Stratoses leading and the rest nowhere, so that after Nicolas's retirement, Rohrl's Kadett took fourth, with Roger Clark's Escort in fifth place. The tyre limitations, incidentally, simply did not help the private owners – but then, only the organisers had expected that they would!

1976

Starting points from Almeria, Copenhagen, Frankfurt, London, Paris, Rome and Warsaw: common route from arrival in Monte Carlo

1. S. Munari – S. Maiga   (Lancia Stratos)
2. B. Waldegard – H. Thorszelius   (Lancia Stratos)
3. B. Darniche – A. Mahe   (Lancia Stratos)
4. W. Rohrl – J. Berger   (Opel Kadett GT/E)
5. R. Clark – J. Porter   (Ford Escort RS1800)
6. M. Alen – I. Kivimaki   (Fiat Abarth 124 Rallye)

163 entries, 148 starters, 84 qualified finishers, 48 completed route

Grand slam
for the Stratos

Although the entry had improved considerably since 1975, the great days of the Monte Carlo seemed to be over. In 1977 the 'works' entry was down to three Lancia Stratoses, four Fiat Abarth 131s, two Opel Kadetts and a selection of Spanish Seats and 'works' Skodas to make up the numbers.

The British, it seemed, had lost interest completely – not only were there no factory Fords, but no British private entrants and (for the first time in half a century) no British start either. Even so, this was yet another occasion when the rally fought back, to gain credibility in future years.

Was it *any* surprise, then, that *Autocar*'s rally report that year was headlined: 'Munari – who else?'. The Lancias, quite clearly, were faster and more effective than any other car in the event, the Italian was seeded at the front of the field, and Lancia's Cesare Fiorio was clearly attracted to the publicity to be gained by three consecutive wins in the world's most famous event, by the same model and the same driver.

When the regulations were published, the routes and the rally's format looked similar to 1976, but three of the proposed 10 starting points were cancelled for lack of custom. In addition to London, the Monte Carlo, Thessalonika (Greece) and Frank-

furt starts were all abandoned. This left Paris (64 starters) by far the most popular on this occasion.

The organisers had abandoned their ridiculous 1976-tyre type limitations, though there were rigidly-applied rules about the number and density of studs which could be used – the French authorities were unhappy about the way that studded tyres damaged road surfaces when all the snow and ice had been worn away.

After the cars congregated on Gap there was usually time for the crews to snatch some rest before they set out to tackle the first of two (it should have been three, but one was cancelled due to a heavy snow fall) stages on the way down to the Mediterranean. The first stage was covered in deep slush and ice for the first (seeded) cars, but warmed up and was gradually swept clear by the passage of cars during the morning – the result was that an unknown French privateer, Alain Beauchef (running at No. 152 in a Ford Escort RS2000) took fastest time ahead of Munari's Lancia.

But not for long. On the next stage the dark-eyed little Italian imposed his will on the event, took the lead and never relinquished it. Munari always seemed to be lucky on this event, for while his team mates (Raffaele Pinto and Bernard Darniche) struck

Oversteer out of this gravelly corner in the 1977 Monte, for Munari, after a spot of understeer getting into the apex. He might have been on the way to winning, and the Stratos was certainly the fastest car in the event, but at high speeds it was a difficult car to drive.

trouble in their identical cars, Munari swept serenely on. Even before the start of the *Parcours Commun* some of the top crews had disappeared. J-P. Nicolas's Opel Kadett blew its engine on the run down from Copenhagen, while Bernard Beguin's Porsche 911 spun on the second stage, the car catching fire and virtually being destroyed.

Up front, as the cars left for the 36-hour run to and from the Ardeche, Munari's Stratos was followed by Guy Frequelin's Alpine-Renault A310, four Fiat 131 Abarths, and two more Lancias. Even so, and in spite of the fog which blanketed the day's first stage, in the next 16 stages the Alitalia-sponsored car was never headed. Darniche's Stratos retired following a crash in a town, Frequelin's Alpine retired when it plunged off the road on black

ice, and Rohrl's Opel Kadett GT/E also retired with a blown engine.

At the Gap rest halt Munari's Lancia led Alen's Fiat 131 Abarth by 41 seconds; some hours later, at the Vals les Bains halt, the gap was still only 42 seconds, but by the time the cars returned to Monte Carlo the lead had stretched to no less than 3 min. 7 sec. The Seats from Spain were going well, if not spectacularly so – but their high finishing positions were only achieved because so many 'works' cars retired in front of them.

On the Mountain Circuit, where 59 cars vied for the privilege of finishing second behind Munari, more of the top teams retired. Pinto's Stratos blew its engine. Markku Alen's Fiat suffered a mysterious electrical problem which cut the engine dead soon

In 1977 Sandro Munari's Lancia Stratos carried Number One, and finished first – his third consecutive victory (fourth in all) on the event.

after the start of the Turini test. Fulvio Bacchelli's Fiat 131 Abarth expired on the Col de la Couillole with a broken drive shaft.

Even Munari's Stratos had electrical trouble at one stage, his lead being dramatically cut by J-C. Andruet's Fiat before the mechanics found, and fixed, the problem. In the end, though, Fiat-Lancia's publicists got their hat-trick. To add to their joy a French girl, Christine Dacremont, also finished sixth and won the Ladies' prize in her Stratos.

1977

Starting points from Almeria, Copenhagen, Lisbon, Paris, Rome and Warsaw: no common route before Monte Carlo

1.	S. Munari – S. Maiga	(Lancia Stratos)
2.	J-C. Andruet – 'Biche'	(Fiat Abarth 131 Rallye)
3.	A. Zanini – A. J. Petisco	(Seat 124 Especial)
4.	S. Canellas – D. Ferrater	(Seat 124 Especial)
5.	G. Swaton – B. Cordesse	(Porsche 911)
6.	Ms. C. Dacremont – Ms. Colette Galli	(Lancia Stratos)

217 entries, 198 starters, 119 qualified finishers, 47 completed route

Someone is going the wrong way here, in 1978 – and there isn't much space to dodge . . .

Private Porsche beats Fiat-Lancia

This was one of the most extraordinary Montes of the modern era. Against all the odds a privately-entered Porsche 911 beat the might of Fiat and Lancia. The Italians had no excuse for being beaten, for all six of their expensively-prepared cars finished the event.

Although the event was well supported, there was a distinct lack of factory teams. The biggest effort, naturally, came from Fiat-Lancia, whose teams had now been combined under the leadership of Cesare Fiorio of Lancia. There were no fewer than four Fiat Abarth 131 saloons, and a brace of Stratos cars from Turin; Michele Mouton also drove a Stratos entered by the French importers.

Facing up to them were two Renault 5 Alpines, a trio of Group One Opel Kadett GT/Es (the troublesome Group Four 16-valve engines having been abandoned) and three diesel-engined Citroën CX2200s from the French factory. Ford, however, chose to stay away, and the only private owner likely to put up a show was ex-Alpine-Renault driver Jean-Pierre ('Jumbo') Nicolas who had a Porsche 911 Carrera, which had been rented from Almeras and was sponsored by Gitanes. There were no British entries.

As in previous years there were limitations on the number of studs which could be used in the tyres, but Pirelli in particular attempted to match this by producing special tyres with different treads and different compounds on each side of the carcases!

After a very uneventful run in to Gap from the eight starting points, the cars re-grouped for the first of the competitive sections on the Monday morning. Between Gap and the first arrival at Monte Carlo, there were five special stages totalling 58 miles/93 km., most of which were covered with deep fresh snow for the first 'seeded' crews.

On that first day the front-wheel-drive Renaults caused something of a sensation, for Jean Ragnotti and Guy Frequelin were always among the top runners, while four-times winner Sandro Munari retired when his Stratos suffered engine failure. Let no-one forget that the Renaults only had 1.4 litre engines and about 130 b.h.p. – they were 're-born Mini-Coopers' and looked splendid where grip was almost non-existent.

For the re-start on the Tuesday morning, with surviving cars ready to tackle a 36-hour run to and from Vals les Bains, which included 133 miles/214 km. of stages, the Renaults led all the 'works' Fiats,

Top photo p.156
In 1978, after the 'works' Fiats had hit all manner of trouble, this was the year of the privateers. Bernard Beguin's car, seen here, broke its gearbox and had to retire, but another 911, driven by Jean-Pierre 'Jumbo' Nicolas, won the event.

Bottom photo p. 156
Chardonnet is the French importer of Lancias and Autobianchi, which explains why this Autobianchi A112 was seen out on the 1978 event. The driver's name – Bruno Saby – was not well-known in those days, but he went on to win the event for Lancia (in the four-wheel-drive Delta) in 1988!

Photo above
The Lancia Stratos won the Monte Carlo four times, but there was no luck in 1978. Two 'works' cars – driven by Sandro Munari and Fulvio Bacchelli – started the event, but Munari's car broke its engine, while Bacchelli's car (seen here) finished tenth, nearly 15 minutes behind the winning Porsche 911.

with Nicolas's Porsche Carrera in fifth place. Fiat, however, seemed set to re-take the initiative by being fastest on the first stage, but Ragnotti's Renault actually overtook Rohrl's Fiat on the next stage and, as the weather around Gap deteriorated into a blizzard, neither the Fiats nor the Lancias ever figured again. On one stage conditions were so bad that one 'works' Fiat was halted and blocked all its team-mates – fortunately the organisers showed good sense (which had been strangely absent in 1973...) and cancelled it!

In the next 24 hours several more stages had to be cancelled, but by the time the cars reached Vals les Bains for the Wednesday morning rest halt, Nicolas's Porsche had moved into the lead ahead of Ragnotti's Renault and Verini's 'works' Fiat Abarth 131. The leading Stratos, driven by Fulvio Bacchelli, was down in 10th place.

By the time the cars returned to Monte Carlo for the second time, Nicolas's Porsche led the two Renaults by 84 sec. and 128 sec. respectively, but with the prospect of much clearer roads on the last nine special stages, to be held over the traditional Mountain Circuit, there was still a chance for the Fiats to make up for their various disasters.

That, at least, was the theory. The practice was that there was enough snow and ice around for the engine-over-driven-wheels cars to keep ahead of the Fiats. Nicolas made no mistakes, nor did the Renaults, and at the end of an exhilarating night's motoring the Porsche's lead over the leading 'works' Fiat – that of Walter Rohrl – had only been reduced from 4 min. 53 sec. to 3 min. 19 sec. Michele Mouton gradually picked up places and took a stirring seventh place in her Lancia Stratos. Anders Kullang won Group One for Opel, which was a great fillip to the team, whose Group Four cars had given them so much grief in previous events.

Although Rohrl's Fiat had set 11 fastest stage times out of 24, against only five fastest times by the Porsche, he along with his team mates had struggled for grip on many other snowy sections. Rohrl's fourth place in the 131 Abarth, nevertheless, was a fine show for a front-engine/rear-wheel-drive car.

1978

Eight starting points: common route from Gap: choice of start point no longer significant.

1. *J-P. Nicolas – V. Laverne*   (Porsche 911)
2. *J. Ragnotti – J-M. Andrie*   (Renault 5 Alpine)
3. *G. Frequelin – J. Delaval*   (Renault 5 Alpine)
4. *W. Rohrl – C. Geistdorfer*   (Fiat Abarth 131 Rallye)
5. *B. Darniche – A. Mahe*   (Fiat Abarth 131 Rallye)
6. *J-C. Andruet – 'Biche'*   (Fiat Abarth 131 Rallye)

216 starters, 134 finished common route, 84 finishers

Escort fortunes on the rocks

Every year, they say, the Monte was memorable for something. In 1979, for sure, there was the 'scandal of the rocks'. Without a stop to move rocks which just 'happened' to be in the road on the penultimate stage, Bjorn Waldegard's Escort RS would have won the event. Victory, thereafter, was handed to a Lancia Stratos. Was it more than coincidence that this car was driven by a Frenchman?

This was the year in which Ford made an all-out (and successful) attempt to win the World Rally Championship, so for the first time since 1976 it entered two very special 272 b.h.p. Escort RS saloons. Compared with 1978, there was a great deal more factory interest, for no fewer than 16 'A-Seed' drivers took part.

Apart from Ford there were four Fiat 131 Abarths (for Alen, Andruet, Michele Mouton and Walter Rohrl), a Stratos for Bacchelli, Fiat Ritmos (Stradas) for Per Eklund and Attilio Bettega, a Renault 5 Alpine for Guy Frequelin, Porsche 911s for 1978-winner J-P. Nicolas and Jacques Almeras himself – and factory-built front-wheel-drive Ford Fiestas for Roger Clark and Ari Vatanen. Ford, naturally, were hoping for relatively clear conditions.

Nicolas's victory in 1978, as a private entry,

encouraged more drivers to enter in 1979, with 233 cars starting from nine European cities. A few crews, including Roger Clark in his Fiesta 1600, started from London, but there was no serious motoring before the various columns joined up at Vals les Bains, where some crews had as much as seven hours' rest.

The run down to Monte Carlo, on the Monday, included five special stages, most of which were clear of snow, though there was quite a lot of slush to be moved by the early runners. It seemed to suit the two 'works' Escorts very well indeed, for Hannu Mikkola was fastest three times and Waldegard once. At Monte Carlo, Mikkola led Waldegard by seven seconds, with Rohrl's and Alen's Fiats a further 20 seconds adrift. At that stage Bernard Darniche, driving the Chardonnet Lancia Stratos, was sixth, 3 min. 7 sec. off the pace.

A total of 197 cars re-started on the Tuesday morning, faced with the by-now very familiar *Parcours Commun*, by way of brief rest halts at Gap and – much later – at Digne. The weather forecast suggested that the remaining snow would clear up, which meant that the spectators could look forward to a good winter 'road race' without many natural hazards.

Renault's front-wheel-drive 5 Alpines were nimble, and effective, when there was a great deal of snow on the ground in the Monte. In 1978 Jean Ragnotti had finished second, but in 1979 (this picture) he had no luck; team-mate Guy Frequelin won the Group 2 category.

In the 15 special stages which followed, the two Ford Escorts pulled further and further away from all their competitors, and the dominance would have been complete if Hannu Mikkola had not cruelly been given a five-minute penalty by the organisers for a traffic offence for 'dangerous passing' on a public road!

Even so, Bjorn Waldegard's car was 4 min. 7 sec.

ahead of Markku Alen's Fiat 131 Abarth, with Rohrl's Fiat a further 19 seconds away. After his unjust penalty, Mikkola was fifth, while the gallant Darniche, in the 'private' Stratos, was no less than 6 min. 27 sec. adrift.

Amazingly, very few cars had retired, so this could certainly be called a straight fight. Even so, with another clear night forecast, for the best 100

160

This was the car with which Ford so nearly won the Monte Carlo Rally 1979. Bjorn Waldegard's 'tarmac-special' Escort RS led until the penultimate stage, when a road blocked by rocks (perhaps placed by vandals) ruined his chances.

cars to tackle the Mountain Circuit, it was clear that tyre technology was going to be important. Ford were on Dunlop, Fiat on Pirelli, and Darniche's Lancia on Michelin.

On the last night there were 10 special stages totalling 109 miles/175 km., and in a modified version of a very familiar format the Turini was to be tackled three times and the Col de Couillole twice. Except for the top of these two stages (where there was some ice), the roads were almost entirely clear. Ford, surely, could not be overhauled?

Darniche thought he had the ideal car, and that he could do it. On the first stage he clawed back 22 seconds, while on the first pass of the Turini he pulled back an astonishing 42 seconds. Dunlop, it was said, had no slick tyres on board – and the

omission was suddenly serious. This duel caused so much excitement that Bacchelli's Stratos retirement (after an accident) and the loss of Rohrl's Fiat with engine failure almost went un-noticed.

With only two stages (and 35 competitive kilometres) to go, the Stratos was still 91 seconds behind. The task looked impossible. Then, running first on the road, Waldegard found the Villars stage blocked by rocks. His co-driver had to get out of the car, run round to the nose, and lever them away before the Escort could continue; Waldegard lost no less than 75 seconds – and, effectively, the rally. On the very last stage Darniche was faster by 21 seconds, and won the event by a mere six seconds.

Was it a famous victory, or a sleazy victory...? We will never know.

Until the last night, Bernard Darniche's Lancia Stratos had no chance of winning the 1979 event. Inspired driving, correct tyre choice, and the infamous 'rocks on the road' scandal all helped give him a six-second victory over Bjorn Waldegard's 'works' Ford Escort RS.

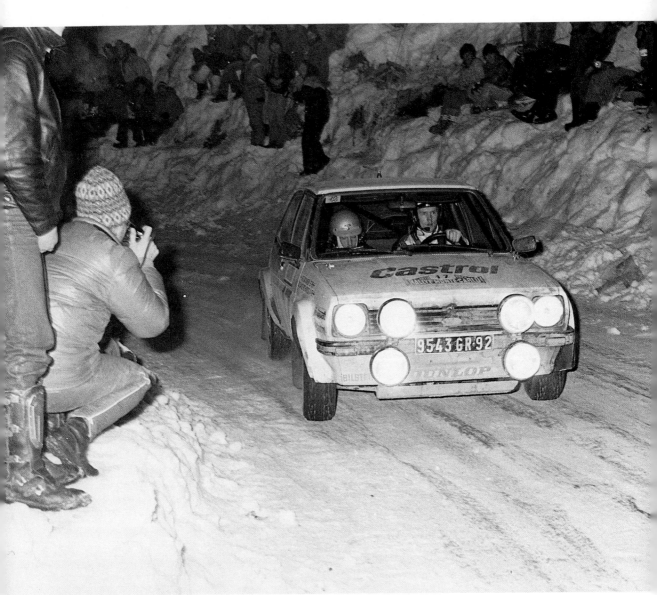

In 1979, Ford not only came close to victory with the 272 b.h.p. Escort RS, but it also entered two front-drive Fiestas. This was Ari Vatanen's car, which finished tenth overall, second in the Group 2 category. Ford soon abandoned the Fiesta, and did not use the car again in the Monte Carlo rally.

1979

Nine starting points: common route from Val le Bains

1. B. Darniche – A. Mahe   (Lancia Stratos)
2. B. Waldegard – H. Thorszelius   (Ford Escort RS)
3. M. Alen – I. Kivimaki   (Fiat Abarth 131 Rallye)
4. J-C. Andruet – Ms. C. Lienard   (Fiat Abarth 131 Rallye)
5. H. Mikkola – A. Hertz   (Ford Escort RS)
6. J-P. Nicolas – J. Todt   (Porsche 911)

233 starters, 154 finished common route, 84 finishers

Fiat's first Monte victory

An easy summary of the 1980 event would surely be – Fiat-Lancia first, the rest nowhere. Compared with 1979 there was no enthralling inter-marque battle for the lead. Instead, here was a clinically efficient demonstration of driving, fine cars and team management. The winning says it all – Walter Rohrl's Fiat 131 Abarth beat Bernard Darniche's Lancia Stratos by more than 10 minutes.

It was, incidentally, the first victory for a front-engine/rear-wheel-drive car since that famous 'steamroller' win by Mercedes-Benz in 1960.

Once again the teams, and the possible winners, had changed. Ford had closed down its motorsport effort to begin developing new cars for the 1980s, which meant that Fiat (with no fewer than five 131 Abarth saloons), Opel (with one of the new Ascona 400 saloons) and Lancia (Darniche's car and a well-driven private entry for François Serbaggi) were sure to make all the running.

There were interesting entries from VW (Golf GTIs, including a car for Per Eklund) and Fiat (a front-drive Ritmo for Attilio Bettega), though Mercedes-Benz preferred to hold back its much-trumpeted return to rallying until Portugal later in the year.

Three cars elected to start in Britain (on this occasion from the Great Danes Hotel, Maidstone) – one being Philip Young and Tony Ambrose in a Morgan Plus Eight, another Noël Francis's Panther Lima, and the third Andy Dawson in a Datsun 160J. Dawson became the event's first retirement, on the short run from Maidstone to Dover, following a contractual dispute with his Japanese masters.

On this occasion the concentrations were only 750 miles/1,200 km. long, the result being that only nine of the 236 hopeful starters fell by the wayside. The real motoring began from the French town of Serre Chevalier, where an ice-test had been laid on for the benefit of French TV.

From Serre Chevalier to Monte Carlo, on the Sunday night, there were six 'proper' special stages in classic Monte Carlo territory, which saw Walter Rohrl jump into an immediate lead. When he went to bed during Monday, he already had a two-minute cushion over Bernard Darniche's Stratos (the driver was suffering from influenza, but kept going), with Bettega's remarkable Fiat Ritmo third and Andruet's Fiat 131 Abarth fourth.

Even at that early point there had been several important retirements – Markku Alen crashed his Fiat on the second stage, Guy Frequelin ('works' Talbot-Sunbeam-Lotus) went off the road two

In 1980 the Fiat 131 Abarth Rallye was at the peak of its success, so the German, Walter Rohrl, drove it to success, thus recording the first of four victories in this classic 'winter' event.

No, this is not the 1930s, but 1980, in which Philip Young and Tony Ambrose tackled the event in a Morgan Plus 8. Unhappily for them, they retired at a very early stage.

stages later, while the German, Achim Warmbold, did the same a few minutes later.

After a 12-hour rest, the column of cars set out to face a *Parcours Commun* in very uncertain weather. Low down, it seemed, there might be wet or dry roads, but at altitude there would certainly be ice and fresh snow. It was a real challenge for the tyre technicians – it being agreed that Pirellis were supreme for snow and ice, but Michelin superior on slush, in the rain, and on dry tarmac.

Walter Rohrl merely settled down to do a professional and completely unflustered job over the

17 stages, and extended his lead considerably. This, incidentally, was in spite of his car suffering a failed ignition pack on a road section (and a 24-minute delay) during that time; somehow he managed to pull back the time.

In the 36-hour marathon (which covered nearly 930 miles/1,500 km.), Hannu Mikkola's Porsche 911 broke a drive shaft, while Ari Vatanen shunted his ex-works Escort RS. As the 125 surviving crews went to bed on the Wednesday, Anders Kullang's newly-homologated Opel Ascona 400 held third place, with Eklund's nimble VW Golf GTI in

After the toil amid the snows, celebration on the seafront at Monte Carlo – Walter Rohrl (right) and Christian Geistdorfer relax on the roof of their 'works' Fiat 131 Abarth Rallye – Rohrl had beaten Bernard Darniche's Lancia Stratos by no less than ten minutes!

second place.

During the final night, where there were 10 special stages to be covered, Rohrl's Fiat merely drove further and further away from all the opposition. Eklund's Golf gradually slipped down the order as bigger and faster cars edged past him, while Andruet's Fiat crashed into a group of spectators. Bernard Darniche had recovered from 'flu and was ready to put on a show. Following Andruet's crash, delays caused three of the 10 stages to be cancelled, so on the Friday morning the lanky West German was pronounced an easy winner.

It had been a convincing win for Fiat, with Rohrl fastest 11 times, second-fastest five times, and third-fastest on another four occasions. Only Bernard Darniche, with 10 fastest times, could approach that.

Nine starting points: common route from Serre Chevalier

1.	W. Rohrl – C. Geistdorfer	(Fiat Abarth 131 Rallye)
2.	B. Darniche – A. Mahe	(Lancia Stratos)
3.	B. Waldegard – H. Thorszelius	(Fiat Abarth 131 Rallye)
4.	A. Kullang – B. Berglund	(Opel Ascona 400)
5.	P. Eklund – H. Sylvan	(VW Golf GTI)
6.	A. Bettega – M. Mannucci	(Fiat Ritmo 75)

236 starters, 125 finishers

1981

The four-wheel-drive era begins

For 1981 there were big changes on the rallying scene – not only in the Monte, but in all other events. The age of the Group Four cars (which had dominated the 1970s) was nearly over, and that of the Group B 'Supercars' was about to begin.

Even so, the 1981 Monte was something of an anti-climax. The new breed of Audi four-wheel-drive cars had been expected to dominate the results – but it was a two-wheel-drive car which won the event. At a casual glance, too, it looked as if an 'ordinary' Renault 5 was victorious.

For 1981, at least, the new cars rubbed shoulders with the old-style Group Four machines. Ford Escort RS, Fiat 131 Abarth and Talbot-Sunbeam-Lotus models were still present, in large numbers, but this time they were being challenged by the newly-successful Opel Ascona 400s, by the mid-engined Renault 5 Turbos, and by the sensational (and controversial) new four-wheel-drive Audi Quattros. Even so, the long-established Porsche 911 design, as driven by Jean-Luc Therier, could not be discounted.

The Renaults and the Quattros made most of the headlines. The Renault, while superficially like that of the 5 from which it took some of its structure, was a purpose-built rally car thought to give ideal balance and traction for the snowy stages of the Alps. The Quattro not only had four-wheel-drive, but also had a *five*-cylinder turbocharged engine. Old-style Fords, Fiats and Talbots made do with 250 b.h.p. and rear-drive, while the Quattros had more than 300 b.h.p. and traction at all four wheels.

The event itself followed the traditional pattern – so much so that some critics were saying that the event was slipping behind the times. There were eight starting points on the Saturday morning, with easy runs of 1,150 km./715 miles leading to a meeting point at Aix-les-Bains a day later.

After sleeping throughout the day, crews were then faced with six special stages on the way to Monte Carlo, another day's (not night's) rest, 18 more stages in the 1,600 km./1,000 mile *Parcours Commun*, a full night's sleep and a day's hanging about, and the final eight stages over the Mountain Circuit itself. Just four crews started from London, none of them likely to be in the top 10, though Graham Newby's Reliant Kitten added spice to a depressingly professional-looking field!

Once again the balance of team power had shifted. Audi, with its four-wheel-drive cars, its mega-budget, and its hiring of Hannu Mikkola and Michele Mouton, was a new force, while Talbot

169

Below

Talbot made a determined attempt to win the rally in 1981, with the thrusting young Henri Toivonen and the more mature Guy Frequelin in two cars. Toivonen, seen here, took fifth place, though Frequelin finished second.

Top photo p.171

1981 was something of an 'interim' year, which gave privately entered cars like Jean-Luc Therier's Porsche 911 a chance to shine – on this occasion, though, he crashed while leading.

Bottom photo p.171

Jean Ragnotti drove the mid-engined/rear-drive Renault 5 Turbo to a very popular victory in 1981. The little car was agile, with great traction – ideal for a rally run in such changeable weather.

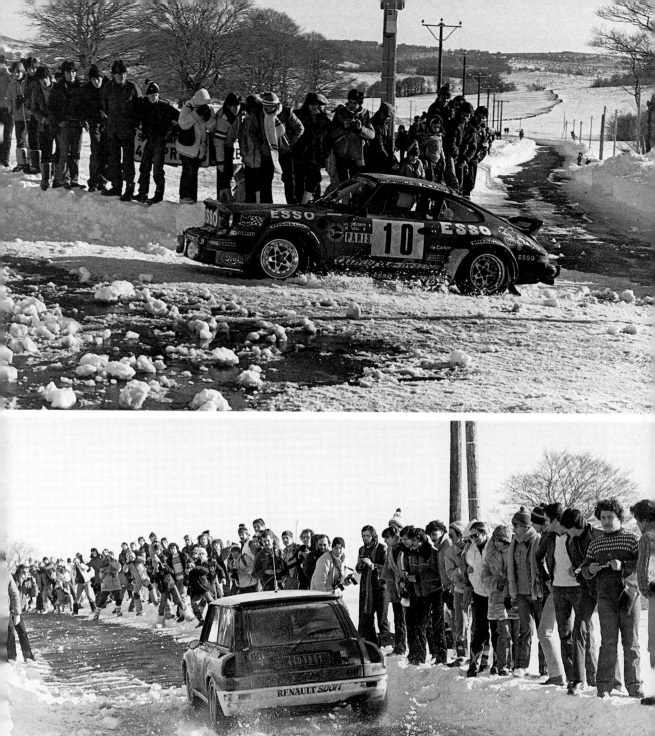

(with Henri Toivonen and Guy Frequelin) and Opel (with Jochi Kleint and Anders Kullang) were also fresh forces. The 'old hands' included Markku Alen in a Fiat 131 Abarth, Bjorn Waldegard and Ari Vatanen in non-factory Escort RSs, Jean Ragnotti and Bruny Saby in Renault 5 Turbos, Bernard Darniche in his faithful old Lancia Stratos, and Jean-Luc Therier in one of the Almeras Porsche 911s.

With tyre and stud regulations even more restricting than ever before (this time they were only allowed to protrude by 2mm from the tread), and with an unpredictable amount of snow on the stages, good traction was going to be hard to find. Audi's challenge faltered, right away, when Michele Mouton's car retired with an engine fuel blockage, but after the Aix-Monte Carlo stages Mikkola's car led by no less than 5 min. 54 sec.!

After that, however, it was all downhill for the German team, for mechanical failures, including the loss of a wheel after an accident, and a further accident, eventually saw the famous Finn pull out of the event.

Therier's Porsche then took over the lead and held it through to the end of the *Parcours Commun*, setting several scintillating fastest times in the process. Ragnotti's Renault (in spite of gearbox problems), Frequelin's Talbot-Sunbeam-Lotus, and Kleint's Opel Ascona 400 all chased strongly, but both Vatanen and Waldegard had a lot of trouble with their Escorts and could not stay on the pace.

For the last night, a 600 km./370 mile thrash on stages more widely scattered than in previous years, Renault screwed up Ragnotti's engine to full-race specification, and the little stunt-man set off, determined to catch Therier's old-style Porsche. After only one stage the chase was over, for Therier put the rear-engined car off the road, and Ragnotti was in the lead, well clear. It was another clear-cut victory for the 'engine-over-driving-wheels' type of car, for none of the front-engine/rear-drive cars could keep up with the Renault.

But then, there had been the colossally fast Quattros on their first-ever World Championship rally. Would they beat everyone in 1982?

1981

Eight starting points: common route from Aix les Bains

    1. *J. Ragnotti – J.M. Andrie* (*Renault 5 Turbo*)
    2. *G. Frequelin – J. Todt* (*Talbot Sunbeam-Lotus*)
    3. *J. Kleint – G. Wanger* (*Opel Ascona 400*)
    4. *A. Kullang – B. Berglund* (*Opel Ascona 400*)
    5. *H. Toivonen – F. Gallagher* (*Talbot Sunbeam-Lotus*)
    6. *B. Darniche – A. Mahe* (*Lancia Stratos*)

263 starters, 133 finishers qualified, 83 completed whole route

Opel
(and the weather)
beat Audi

According to the pundits this, the 50th Monte Carlo rally, should have seen the first victory by a four-wheel-drive car, but the weather man had better ideas. When Audi's team saw the state of the roads immediately before the start of the 1982 event, their hearts must have sunk. To win, what the Quattro really needed was snow and ice – lots of it – but the roads were almost clear. It was a time for team-leader Hannu Mikkola to grit his teeth, push the bulky four-wheel-drive car as hard as he could, and hope that the opposition would break down.

It did not. Although the Quattro set 10 fastest and eight second-fastest times in the 34-stage event, Walter Rohrl's Opel Ascona 400 (newly-sponsored by Rothmans) was faster and more versatile. At the end of a fast event, held mostly in balmy weather, the rear-drive Opel beat the four-wheel-drive Audi by nearly four minutes. Jean-Luc Therier's Almeras team Porsche 911SC was a further eight minutes adrift, and no-one else was close.

The new wave of rallying regulations – Groups N, A and Group B replacing Groups One, Two, Three and Four – were to run in parallel with the old rules for a while, which meant that this Monte was still basically a 'Group Four' event. Compared with 1981, the 1982 entry looked very different. The only 'works' efforts came from Audi (three Quatros) and Opel (two Asconas 400s). There were no Fords, no Fiats, no Talbots and no Renaults; in some cases these teams had decided not to compete against the might of Audi (whose Quattro had started winning World Championship rallies towards the end of 1981), in others they were getting on with the design of new Group B cars. To add to the interest, Jean-Claude Andruet drove a beautifully-prepared Ferrari 308GTB, but this was to crash after only four special stages.

Once again there were eight starting points, and once again the UK (with just three cars starting from Dover) was almost ignored. The organisers had given their event a more thorough shake-out than in previous years, for between Aix-les-Bains and the first arrival in Monte Carlo there were to be 10 special stages, there would be more than four hours of flat-out motoring in the *Parcours Commun*, while the final night's run stretched from Monte Carlo to Digne and back, taking in 10 special stages and a total of 705 km./440 miles.

Walter Rohrl had been virtually out of rallying for a year, after his much-hyped deal with Mercedes-Benz was cancelled, but came back with a bang on this Monte, driving for the Opel 'works' team. Right

On the 1982 event Guy Frequelin drove an Almeras-prepared Porsche 911 (a generously-financed, but essentially private, entry) into fourth place, immediately behind his team mate Jean-Luc Therier.

In 1982 there was so little snow that the conventional (front-engined/rear-drive) Opels always had the legs of the Audis. Walter Rohrl beat Mikkola's Quattro by four minutes to record his second victory in the event.

from the start, on roads which were ideal for the large but nimble Ascona 400, he was the standard-setter. Guy Frequelin's Almeras Porsche 911 led after the first stage of all, but after the first 10 stages had been completed, Rohrl had set a series of fastest times and was already in command. Mikkola's Quattro had suffered punctures and a broken drive shaft; he was being beaten by team-mate Michele Mouton who was in fourth place.

On the long run out from Monte Carlo to Vals-les-Bains, on the *Parcours Commun*, there were only patches of ice to encourage the Audis, and except that Rohrl once made a super-cautious tyre choice and was actually caught on a stage by team-mate Jochi Kleint, the Opel driver was never troubled. It was a very out-of-character Monte where slick racing tyres were almost always chosen for the stages!

On this section Michele Mouton crashed her Quattro, while Kleint suffered punctures, and would eventually put his Opel off the road for a time, dropping from second to seventh place, while Frequelin's Porsche held on grimly to third place. Mikkola's first night disasters were behind him, but he was always aiming for second, not first, place.

On the last night, Rohrl rubbed in his superiority by being fastest on the first two stages of the night, then sharing a further five fastest times with team-mate Kleint on the final stages. He beat Mikkola's Audi on all but two occasions – it was no wonder that Mikkola threw in the towel, eased back, and finished four minutes behind.

Right from the start this had been a two-car race, so the exploits of the old-fashioned Porsches tended to be ignored. Even so, Guy Frequelin set five fastest stage times – three of them on the last night – while two privately-entered Renault 5 Turbos finished strongly in fifth and sixth places.

Audi would have to try again – all over again – in 1983.

1982

Eight starting points: common route from Aix les Bains

1.	W. Rohrl – C. Geistdorfer	*(Opel Ascona 400)*
2.	H. Mikkola – A. Hertz	*(Audi Quattro)*
3.	J-L. Therier – M. Vial	*(Porsche 911SC)*
4.	G. Frequelin – J-F. Fauchille	*(Porsche 911SC)*
5.	B. Saby – Ms. F. Sappey	*(Renault 5 Turbo)*
6.	D. Snobeck – Ms. D. Emanuelli	*(Renault 5 Turbo)*

299 starters, 140 qualified finishers, 91 complete route

Lancia's 'racer' beats Audi's monster

Audi had failed to win the Monte in 1981, but came close to victory in 1982. Surely nothing could stop them in 1983? Surely that prestigious rally victory would not be denied them? The fates, however, were still not on Audi's side. Not only were the roads almost completely clear of snow and ice, but Lancia's new Group B car, the mid-engined Rally 037, was a formidably competitive machine.

For 1983, rallying's famous names, and famous faces, had changed around. Although Walter Rohrl had won the World Rally Championship for Opel in 1982, he had been so unhappy with the team's sponsors (Rothmans) that he had left after only one year to join the Lancia team. Ari Vatanen and Henri Toivonen had stayed with Opel, joined now by Guy Frequelin, while Stig Blomqvist had come out of the rallying 'wilderness' to drive for Audi. The 'new' drivers for Audi, Opel and Lancia all defeated their more established team-mates!

The big battles in 1983, therefore, would be between Audi's Quattros, Opel's Asconas and Mantas and Lancia's Rally 037s, though the Opels were not expected to be competitive on loose-surfaced events. The line-up for the Monte reflected this, for there were three 'works' Quattros, three Lancias and three Opels. Also in the large entry there

was a new Nissan 240RS for Timo Salonen, and Renault 5 Turbos for 1981 winner Jean Ragnotti, and for Jean-Luc Therier and Bruno Saby, but the rest of the large entry were make-weights. It was interesting to see that more and more pressure-charged engines were coming into use, though four-wheel-drive competition for Audi was still not ready. This was the first Monte, incidentally, in which the old Groups Two and Four were banned – like other World Championship events in 1983, Groups N, A and B were dominant.

Once again there were changes to the format. Seven starting points attracted 250 cars, of which just seven elected to begin from Dover. After only 1,295 km./805 miles the crews met up at Grenoble, spent much of the day in bed, then tackled a 615 km./382 mile *Classement* run to Monte Carlo, a route which included five special stages.

After a day's rest it was time for the first 200 cars to tackle the Monte-Vals-les-Bains-Monte run, with 15 stages in 1,581 km./983 miles, then after a further night's rest the survivors had to do a final 10 stages in the mountains. The Mountain Circuit was a little more compact and concentrated than in 1982, for five stages (including the famous Turini) were all used twice.

Photo above

In 1983 the Monte weather was too good for the Quattros, which could not use the grip of their four-wheel-drive systems. Stig Blomqvist drove his heart out, though, to finish third behind the two 'works' Lancias.

Top photo, p.179

Open wide, please! The mid-engined Lancia Rally 037 of Francis Serpaggi (who finished ninth) being fettled in the 1983 event. The Rally 037 was an out-and-out competition car, as this study makes clear.

Bottom photo, p.179

Jean Ragnotti, victor in 1981, could only achieve seventh in 1983, a year in which the weather was kind, and in which Walter Rohrl's mid-engined Lancia Rally 037 was dominant.

The roads in the Chartreuse had some icy patches, and in the first five stages the honours were shared – one fastest time to Therier's Renault, two to Blomqvist's Quattro, and one each to Alen's and Rohrl's Lancias. Conditions were so variable that Lancia even found the opportunity to mount one of its famous 'tyre pit stops' in the middle of a stage!

At the re-start, Rohrl's Lancia was already ahead of his team-mates Markku Alen and Jean-Claude Andruet, and Hannu Mikkola was struggling to keep up with Stig Blomqvist, who actually led the rally at this point. Opel's Asconas, frankly, were outclassed, both on performance and traction grounds – Walter Rohrl's defection after only one season was soon seen to be wise.

As the *Parcours Commun* proceeded, the Lancias became more and more dominant. Although there were a few retirements to upset the order (Michele Mouton crashed her Quattro – which made it twice in two years – as did Guy Frequelin his Ascona), things soon settled down, with Walter Rohrl's Lancia ahead of Andruet and Alen (also in Lancias). Andruet would later fall back following a Lancia engine supercharger failure, but he still stayed in touch. The German was taking so much time out of Blomqvist's chasing Audi that it was almost embarrassing – 30 or 40 seconds, even more than a minute being a normal gap. This event was not about traction, but about power-weight ratios and race-car handling. Not even a three-hour halt at Vals-les-Bains could alter this.

Before the start of the Mountain Circuit, all the drivers were convinced that the rally was won and lost. Even though there were reports of some snow, and some ice patches, these were scarce, and few of the usually spectacular rally pictures had evidence of the white stuff on the ground.

At the end of the night, in which Lancias were fastest on seven of the 10 stages (Toivonen's and Vatanen's Opels clocked up one fastest each, along with one fastest time for Blomqvist's Quattro), there was no significant change. Two Lancias finished ahead of two Quattros, with two Opel Asconas behind them – which summed things up perfectly. Between them, the Lancia drivers had set 23 fastest times on the 31 stages, and it was Walter Rohrl's third victory, using three different types of car. *That* was total domination.

1983

Seven starting points: common route from Grenoble

1. W. Rohrl – C. Geistdorfer   (Lancia Rally 037)
2. M. Alen – I. Kivimaki   (Lancia Rally 037)
3. S. Blomqvist – B. Cederberg   (Audi Quattro)
4. H. Mikkola – A. Hertz   (Audi Quattro)
5. A. Vatanen – T. Harryman   (Opel Ascona 400)
6. H. Toivonen – F. Gallagher   (Opel Ascona 400)

250 starters, 148 qualified finishers, 88 completed route

Quattro domination in real Monte weather

At the fourth attempt, Audi's Quattro finally won the Monte Carlo rally for which it had usually been favourite to succeed. In 1984 the weather was properly seasonal – with ice, wet snow or dry snow on all stages, rain or snow falling most of the time, and with two special stages actually cancelled before the cars arrived – due to blizzard conditions. One thing, however, did not change – it was an event dominated by Walter Rohrl who had once again changed teams!

The coldly analytical Rohrl had enjoyed his year with Lancia, but finished second to Hannu Mikkola (Audi Quattro) in the World Drivers' Championship. Accordingly, to improve on that situation he signed for Audi in 1984! The A2 Quattro was a better car in 1984 than it had been in 1983, and its first performance of the year, on the Monte Carlo rally, proved it.

Although the Monte's 'Top Ten' driver list was a star-studded affair, there were few competitive cars in the field. Audi entered three Quattros for Rohrl, Mikkola and Blomqvist, to fight Lancia's team of Alen, Andruet, Bettega and Biasion in Rally 037s. The Audis produced about 360 b.h.p., and the Lancias 325 b.h.p. However, except for Timo Salonen's underpowered Nissan 240RS, and

Therier's Renault 5 Turbo, that was the end of the competitive cars which might be expected to fight for the lead. The top drivers reckoned that Lancia would only be able to match Audi if less than 30 per cent of the stages were snow covered.

Other 'works' teams had abandoned attempts to win the rally – not only because of the cost of competing (a mountain of tyre choice, and the need for cohorts of ice-notes crews to keep the star drivers informed of weather conditions), but because of the unwieldy nature of the route.

In spite of complaints from entrants, the organisers refused to cut down the sprawling nature of the route, though at least there would only be two long competitive sections in the 1984 event. There were eight starting points, as far-flung as London and Barcelona, but 1,200 km./750 miles later the crews all congregated at Aix-les-Bains. However, for the first time in many years, most of the competitive sections would be over before the cavalcade even reached Monte Carlo for the first time.

After a suitable rest in the ancient French town, they tackled a *Parcours Commun* of 20 special stages and 1,580 km./980 miles, which led direct to Monte Carlo. Twenty-four hours later the traditional Mountain Circuit, of 10 stages, would complete the

Top photo, p.182
Bernard Darniche set a stirring pace in the 1984 rally in his Group A Audi 80 Quattro, winning the category and finishing seventh overall.

Bottom photo, p.182
Although Lancia's Rally 037 had won in 1983, it was outpaced by the Quattros in 1984. Attilio Bettega drove this, the highest-placed Lancia, and finished fifth overall.

Photo above
Team celebrations, in 1984, for Audi, whose four-wheel-drive Quattros notched up a 1-2-3 result. The winner, Walter Rohrl, is waving the champagne bottle, with second-man Stig Blomqvist to his left, and third-man Hannu Mikkola to the left of Blomqvist. It was Rohrl's fourth Monte success.

event. Even in mild weather this was a daunting route, for there were 722 km./449 miles of stages, but on this occasion, with the weather worsening by the hour as the cars arrived in Aix-les-Bains, it began to look like a four-wheel-drive benefit.

Right from the start, Audi were dominant. After five special stages, with the cars on the west side of the Rhône valley, Messrs. Blomqvist, Rohrl and Mikkola occupied the first three places. Two Renault 5 Turbos – driven by Jean-Luc Therier and Bruno Saby – were already three minutes behind, while Markku Alen's and Attilio Bettega's rear-drive Lancias were no fewer than 6 min. 30 sec. off the pace. Lancia's choice of racing tyres, on a stage where fresh snow fell immediately *after* the choice was made, didn't help.

During the Tuesday night the weather got progressively worse. Walter Rohrl's Quattro set a string of 11 fastest times, so that when the cars arrived in Monte Carlo, having completed 16 stages (four of the first 20 were cancelled, mostly due to the blizzard conditions), he led team-mate Blomqvist by 29 seconds, but the best of the two-wheel-drive cars (Therier's Renault 5 Turbo) was fourth, and no less than 18 *minutes* adrift.

In more ways than one, this was a 'whitewash' for Audi, who had waited three long years for such a sweet experience. *This* was what Roland Gumbert had planned for in 1980, and *this* was why Hannu Mikkola had turned down other lucrative offers to sign for Audi in 1980.

It was the same story, with just as much emphasis, on the last night. Five stages had to be tackled twice each and, although there was much more clear road than on the *Parcours Commun*, it was still ideal Quattro territory. Rohrl's car was fastest four times, matched by four fastest times from Stig Blomqvist. Only Attilio Bettega (Lancia Rally 037), fastest on each of the runs over the clear-road Col de la Madonie, offered spirited resistance.

At the end of the event, Walter Rohrl only beat Stig Blomqvist's sister car by 73 seconds, but he was no less than 24 min. 24 sec. ahead of Therier's two-wheel-drive Renault. For Lancia it was complete humiliation – for Bettega's Rally 037 was almost 30 *minutes* off the pace. What a difference a year makes!

1984

Eight starting points: common route from Aix les Bains

1. W. Rohrl – C. Geistdorfer   (Audi Quattro)
2. S. Blomqvist – B. Cederberg   (Audi Quattro)
3. H. Mikkola – A. Hertz   (Audi Quattro)
4. J-L. Therier – M. Vial   (Renault 5 Turbo)
5. A. Bettega – M. Perissinot   (Lancia Rally 037)
6. M. Biasion – T. Siviero   (Lancia Rally 037)

209 starters, 120 qualified finishers, 75 complete route

Peugeot's 205T16 takes charge

Although Audi's Quattro had been a stunning success in its early years, other and more advanced four-wheel-drive cars where developed to beat it. Peugeot unveiled its new mid-engined Group B monster, the 205T16, during 1984 and in 1985 – its very first assault on the Monte Carlo rally – it won the event outright, 53 years since its previous win. Those who knew the ruthless resolve of Peugeot's motorsport supremo, Jean Todt, expected nothing less.

The Quattro victory in the 1984 Monte had brought all two-wheel-drive 'winter' rally successes to an end. For the 1985 rally, therefore, no-one without four-wheel-drive could hope to win. Even so, Lancia, whose own 4WD design was still not ready, brought out its rear-drive Rally 037s yet again.

Once again, the quality of the entry was rather 'thin'. There were three of the new transverse-mid-engined Peugeots, for Ari Vatanen, Timo Salonen and Bruno Saby, facing up to two of the latest short-wheelbase Audi Quattro Sports, which were being driven by Walter Rohrl and Stig Blomqvist. Jean-Claude Andruet, Maurice Chomat and Philippe Wambergue were entered in diminutive four-wheel-drive Citroën Visa Mille Pistes models, while

Lancia's obsolete Rally 037s were driven by Henri Toivonen and Miki Biasion. Power outputs were still on the way up, for the Peugeots and the Audis had between 400 and 450 b.h.p., the Lancia 'only' 340 b.h.p. Except for Danny Snobeck's privately-entered Renault 5 Turbo, no other car had a remote chance of success.

This was a Monte Carlo rally almost smothered by political intrigue before it could start, for there was acrimonious disagreement on 'political' grounds between the Monegasques and FISA. Happily, the dispute was all resolved in December 1984, just in time for a typical winter race to be held. Even so, many potential entrants had scrapped plans to compete by that time, and in the end only 117 crews faced the starter's flag – the lowest figure since the 'post-scandal' year of 1975.

The route, over the years, was gradually contracting into a more sensible and compact layout. This time there were only six starting points, 1,000 km./620 miles from the common meeting point at St. Etienne. The British starting point had finally been abandoned, the most remote from Monte Carlo itself being Bad Hombourg in West Germany, and Barcelona in Spain.

From St. Etienne there was a five-stage Clas-

Peugeot set out to build a dominant four-wheel-drive Group B car in 1982, started rallying it in 1983, and saw Ari Vatanen use this car to win the 1985 Monte Carlo Rally. A famous victory...

By the 1980s the rally attracted spectators from all round Europe to watch the cars on special stages. These hardy enthusiasts had been waiting for hours in 1985 to see their favourites slither by.

Ceremonial start for Ari Vatanen and Terry Harryman's Peugeot 205T16, from the Eiffel Tower, in Paris, on the 1985 event. They went on to win the event, with other such Peugeots third and fifth overall.

sification run to Grospierres, followed after a night's rest by an 18-stage *Parcours Commun* through Grenoble and Gap to Monte Carlo itself. The final challenge was the 11-stage Mountain Circuit, held on the Thursday night, which included all the old favourites – Col de la Madonie, Col du Turini, Col St. Sauveur and Col St. Raphael. It was an event where supreme team organisation and, above all, correct 'ice-noting' and choice of tyres, was going to pay off. There had been a lot of snow until a week before the event, but then came a thaw and conditions gradually improved – unhappily for Lancia, though, not by enough!

The odds were always against Audi, whose new short-wheelbase car was fast but unwieldy, but no-one was willing to write off Walter Rohrl and Stig Blomqvist in this event. Even after the opening stages, the order had settled down, with Ari Vatanen's nimble Peugeot being driven harder than that of his team-mate Timo Salonen, with Rohrl's Quattro Sport struggling to stay on terms, and with the Lancias losing 30 seconds to one minute on the longer stages. The miracle, though, was that few cars were dropping out, neither accidents nor mechanical breakdowns rife.

At Grospierres, after five partly-clear stages, Rohrl's Quattro actually led Vatanen by 35 seconds, with Henri Toivonen's Lancia another 49 seconds adrift, but from that moment onwards the Lancia was in trouble. Toivonen lost 61 sec. on the next stage, and no less than 2 min. 42 sec. on the 45 km. Burzet loop. Ari Vatanen's Peugeot overhauled Rohrl's Quattro before the Grenoble rest halt (after 12 stages), after which there were no important changes in position.

Just when Peugeot was beginning to relax, however, Vatanen's co-driver Terry Harryman made a mistake when clocking in to a control at Gap. At the stroke his four-minute lead became a four-minute deficit, leaving the blond Finn (as the athletics commentators would say) with 'everything to do'.

This was the inspiration for one of Vatanen's finest performances, for over the remaining 16 special stages the 'flying Finn' set fastest time on 11 occasions, taking great chunks out of Rohrl's lead. The lanky German led by 1 min. 58 sec. before the final night, but was overhauled in just three stages; dispirited by Peugeot's effortless progress, he could do nothing, and a four-minute halt due to electrical failure didn't help his cause.

All in all, Vatanen's T16 was fastest on 21 of the 34 stages. Please note, too, that *without* his road penalty, Vatanen would have beaten Rohrl by 13 minutes . . .

1985

Six starting points: common route from St. Etienne

1. A. Vatanen – T. Harryman (Peugeot 205T16)
2. W. Rohrl – C. Geistdorfer (Audi Sport Quattro)
3. T. Salonen – S. Harjanne (Peugeot 205T16)
4. S. Blomqvist – B. Cederberg (Audi Sport Quattro)
5. B. Saby – J-F. Fauchille (Peugeot 205T16)
6. H. Toivonen – J. Piironen (Lancia Rally 037)

117 starters, 87 qualified finishers, 68 completed route

A Group B
Supercar
spectacular

This, without doubt, was the most spectacular Monte Carlo rally of all time. This was the event in which several teams of the new-generation four-wheel-drive Group B 'Supercars' battled, head-to-head, in which speeds were higher than ever before, but in which Lancia's sensational turbo/super-charged Delta S4 won at its first attempt. We did not know it then, but there was not to be another Eighties' Monte Carlo rally like this.

It had taken time for the world's manufacturers to develop their new Group B cars. All, without exception, had four-wheel-drive, and all were extremely powerful, but there were still many solutions to the same problem. Peugeot 205T16 was already a World Champion, Audi's be-winged Quattro Sport S1 was obsolescent, while Citroëns' new BX4TC was front-engined and unwieldy. Austin-Rover's Metro 6R4 was normally-aspirated and hideous, Lancia's Delta was as technically advanced as we had expected – and Ford's pretty RS200 was not yet homologated!

For the Monte, therefore, there was a phe-nomenal 'works' entry – four Peugeots faced up to two Audis, three Lancia Deltas, two MG Metro 6R4s and two big Citroëns. The total entry was larger than in 1985, but in truth few were interested

in what was happening behind the first 20 cars! In every way this was going to be a gladiatorial, hi-tech race for supremacy, where highly-paid drivers were only the tip of a team's big-spending efforts.

To match this phenomenal entry the organisers re-jigged their rally to present an even greater challenge. From six starting points there was merely an easy 1,000 km./620 mile-run to Aix-les-Bains, a brief rest halt to re-group, then the competition began in earnest. First off there was the six-stage Classification run, from Aix to Aix, including classic trials like the ascent of Mont Revard and the 44 km. passage of the Chartreuse stage (actually the reverse run over the Cols de Porte, Cucheron and Granier, which had been a Monte favourite for many years).

A night halt in Aix was followed by the gruelling 1,750 km./1,090-mile *Parcours Commun* run to Monte Carlo, which included 18 stages, many of them over 30 km. in length, by way of controls at Vienne, Grospierres, Vaison-le-Romaine and Gap. Finally, there was the 11-stage Mountain circuit on the Thursday night, very similar indeed to that used in previous years.

All in all there were 36 stages totalling 867 km./539 miles. The fastest cars were expected to take more than 10 hours to complete these stages – it

The Lancia Delta S4's first, and only, Monte Carlo run came in 1986, when Henri Toivonen won the event outright, in spite of crashing into a spectator's car and damaging the chassis of the four-wheel-drive Supercar.

was going to be the supreme test of men and machinery.

For some teams – Citroën and Austin-Rover in particular – there was nothing but trouble, but for the others there was exhilarating competition. Both the big Citroëns dropped out after six stages, Tony Pond's Metro completed only the same number, and Malcolm Wilson's Metro broke its transmission soon afterwards.

As the competitive motoring got under way, the weather began to improve and most of the later special stages were either clear or covered with wet

snow or ice patches. It was a difficult challenge for the tyre companies, resolved in favour of Pirelli (and Lancia!). After the first six snowy stages, therefore, Henri Toivonen's 450 b.h.p. Lancia Delta S4 led team-mate Markku Alen by 65 seconds, with Miki Baision's Delta 12 seconds further away. Then came Saby's Peugeot, Rohrl's 'second evolution' Quattro Sport, Salonen's Peugeot, Mikkola's Quattro, and Michele Mouton's Peugeot. Tony Pond's Metro had already suffered from steering failure, and was withdrawn by the team's management.

Andruet's Citroën had trouble in re-starting

One of the most exciting Montes of all was held in 1986, when the Group B 'Supercars' were all tremendously fast. 1985 World Champion Timo Salonen (Peugeot 205T16) battled it out with Lancia's Henri Toivonen, but could only finish second, four minutes off the pace.

from *parc fermé*, but the rest of the Group B cars then headed west and south for the 'meat' of the event. Except that Timo Salonen's Peugeot overhauled Miki Baision's Lancia there were no immediate changes to the order, but then the mechanical dramas began. Saby's Peugeot suffered a turbo fire, Kankkunen's Peugeot had fuel feed troubles, Rohrl's Quattro suffered a misfire, then a puncture which had to be changed in mid-stage; this cost him six minutes and effectively put him out of contention. Worst of all, the rally leader, Henri Toivonen, hit a non-competing car on a road section and suffered a

badly handling, damaged car for the rest of the event.

Before the Mountain Circuit began, Timo Salonen's Peugeot was narrowly in the lead by 33 seconds, in spite of Lancia's mid-stage tyre-changing tactics at one point. On the final night, however, when there was very little snow (the top of the Turini was almost clear), Henri Toivonen's strange-handling Delta set six fastest times out of 11 stages, whereas Salonen was fastest only twice. Henri, who was to be so tragically killed in Corsica a few months later, emulated his equally famous father, who had won that controversial 1966 event exactly 20 years earlier.

Henri Toivonen (right) and Sergio Cresto on the roof of their victorious Lancia Delta S4 after winning the 1986 event. Tragically, Henri lost his life in a crash in the Tour de Corse a few months later.

1986

Six starting points: common route from Aix-les-Bains

1. H. Toivonen – S. Cresto   (Lancia Delta S4)
2. T. Salonen – S. Harjanne   (Peugeot 205T16)
3. H. Mikkola – A. Hertz   (Audi Sport Quattro)
4. W. Rohrl – C. Geistdorfer   (Audi Sport Quattro)
5. J. Kankkunen – J. Piironen   (Peugeot 205T16)
6. B. Saby – J-F. Fauchille   (Peugeot 205T16)

156 starters, 85 qualified finishers, 65 completed route

1987

Lancia wins the first 'Group A' Monte

Two disasters shocked the world of rallying into major changes in 1986 – a Ford RS200 plunged into a crowd in Portugal in March, and Henri Toivonen's Lancia crashed in Corsica a few weeks later. In both cases violent death followed. The result was that Group B cars were banned from rallying from the end of the year, and the events themselves were made less demanding.

For 1987, therefore, the Monte was 'de-tuned', in several ways. The event was now to be organised for Group A and Group N cars, both of which had to be built at the rate of 5,000 cars a year, where the most powerful machine was Ford's 300 b.h.p. Sierra RS Cosworth. Special stage lengths were cut considerably, the result being that the 1987 event included 'only' 572 km./356 miles of stages, well down on the previous year. There was another fundamental change – that all but two of the stages were held in daylight.

Was this, therefore, the shape of Monte Carlo rallies for the future? If so, some things had not changed at all. There were still five starting points, this time with a meeting point at Grenoble; there was still a Classification run (a loop around Grenoble); there was still a long (1,375 km./855-mile) *Parcours Commun* towards Monte Carlo; and there was still a

Mountain Circuit on the Thursday. In total there were only 25 stages, and the major upheaval was that the Mountain Circuit had only a single loop, five stages, and was held during daylight hours.

The cars, of course, were completely different. Because Group B had been cancelled so abruptly, few 'traditional' rallying manufacturers had new Group A cars ready for use – and in any case design and development of special new 5,000-off models was going to be a more complex business than it had been for the 200-off Group B formula.

Lancia – who else? – *was* ready, with the four-wheel-drive Delta HF 4WD hatchback, most fortuitously put on sale during 1986. There were those who said that there had always been a fully-fledged Group A programme, others who insisted that it was merely a happy coincidence... Audi fell back on its big 200 Quattro saloon (which used similar chassis components to the banned Group B cars), Mazda brought its existing Group A 323 Turbo 4WD into the limelight, VW decided to soldier on with its front-drive Golf GTIs, while Ford found it difficult to decide between under-powered Sierra XR4×4 (four-wheel-drive) or Sierra RS Cosworth (rear-wheel-drive) cars. All were present on this, the first Group A Monte, and all had high hopes.

Miki Biaison won the 1987 event in the new Group A Lancia Delta HF 4WD, but only after 'team orders' had been applied by team chief Cesare Fiorio.

Some teams – notably Peugeot, Austin-Rover and Citroën – were not present at all. A lot, indeed, had changed in just 12 months.

The event was one of the snowiest on record yet, because of the much-reduced power of the competing cars and it was one of the least spectacular to watch. Most of the excitement was generated behind the scenes – immediately when Mazda's Achim Warmbold unsuccessfully protested against Lancia's interpretation of the homologations, and later when Stig Blomqvist's Sierra XR4×4 lost its fourth place because of homologation anomalies.

Lancia, with team drivers Miki Baision, Juha Kankkunen and Bruno Saby, were so dominant that they were fastest on all but eight stages, and this with only 240 b.h.p. Team boss Cesare Fiorio even applied 'team orders' towards the finish, insisting that Miki Baision should win, though Kankunnen was demonstrably the faster driver! Every other team, and car, was struggling. Walter Rohrl drove the big and heavy Audi as fast as it could be moved (and set five fastest stage times in the process), Stig Blomqvist achieved miracles with the underpowered Sierra, while Mazda (with Timo Salonen and Ingvar

Even with the aid of modern tyres (and a helping push from spectators!) some front-engined/rear-drive cars find grip hard to find. 1979 winner Bernard Darniche in trouble in 1987, in his Mercedes-Benz 190E 2.3-16.

Carlsson driving) wondered when they would have reliability to go with good handling and compact dimensions.

Right from the start, Lancia was dominant, with Bruny Saby leading at first, and Miki Biasion taking over on the fourth stage. Mazda was in trouble keeping its engine turbo pipes in place, while Rohrl was complaining that his big Audi felt 'like rallying 15 years ago'; it was certainly heavy enough – for the FISA scales rated it at 1,372 kg./3,025 lb.!

After 10 stages, with the cars at the Aubenas rest halt, the order had settled down – three Lancias,

Rohrl's Audi and Blomqvist's Ford – and except that Saby's Lancia would shortly drop out with a broken transmission, that was that for the next two days.

Once the Lancias had eased off, there was no contest remaining, and after Fiorio decreed that the time over the Turini test should govern the winner it was all over bar the complaining. There was plenty of that – Juha Kankkunen thought he had been robbed, and so did Mazda!

The rest of the 1987 season would go much the same way . . .

1987

Five starting points – Bad Homburg, Barcelona, Lausanne, Monte Carlo and Sestriere: common route from Grenoble

1. *M. Biasion – T. Siviero* (Lancia Delta HF 4WD)
2. *J. Kankkunen – J. Piironen* (Lancia Delta HF 4WD)
3. *W. Rohrl – C. Geistdorfer* (Audi 200 Quattro)
4. *S. Blomqvist – B. Berglund* (Ford Sierra XR4×4)★★
5. *I. Carlsson – P. Carlsson* (Mazda 323 4WD Turbo)
6. *K. Eriksson – P. Diekmann* (VW Golf GTI 16V)
7. *J. Ragnotti – P. Thimonier* (Renault 11 Turbo)

160 starters, 94 finishers

★★ *Later disqualified for homologation infringement*

Another Lancia Delta walkover

In 1987, Lancia's domination of the World Championship rally scene had been so complete that some of the Italian company's rivals simply gave up the chase. Audi withdrew from the sport, Ford sidelined the four-wheel-drive Sierra because it was short of power, while Mazda's fortunes were wrecked by a scandal over homologation.

For the 1988 Monte Carlo rally, therefore, the *only* worthwhile competition for Lancia came from Mazda, whose Brussels-based team had tried to shrug off the problems of 1987, were using a stronger optional transmission, and had even persuaded Hannu Mikkola to join the team to boost the driving strength. Oreille's Renault 11 Turbo was not really a fully-fledged 'works' car, and there were no serious entries from Peugeot or Citroën.

It was, in other words, almost a guaranteed walkover for Lancia, a company which was not about to abdicate the winner's rostrum merely because it had little competition! Accordingly, three brand-new Delta HF 4WD cars were entered for Bruno Saby, Yves Loubet and Miki Biaison, less powerful than at the end of the 1987 season (following rule changes affecting engine intercooler sizes), but still with about 240 b.h.p. as in the 1987 event. Mazda (with cars driven by Hannu Mikkola, Timo Salonen

and Ingvar Carlsson) was pointing to the use of a strong six-speed gearbox as the reason for its optimism, though the 1.6 litre engines only had about 220 b.h.p.

From five starting points (was this the beginning of the end for the 'far-flung' Monte run-in sections?) the cars congregated at St. Etienne before tackling stages on the way to Aubenas and the first-night halt. Ice-notes crews revealed that there was little snow on the stages, and that much of what *was* there had been shovelled down from the banks by 'enthusiasts' to make the stages more interesting. As one rallying pundit later pointed out, one or two of the Ford Sierra RS Cosworths, or the BMW M3s, idle during January, might have been very competitive indeed on *this* Monte!

Mazda's rally started badly, when both 'works' cars were dramatically slowed by fuelling problems, later found to be due to the contamination of petrol by diesel fuel! Mikkola's car disappeared after only three stages with this problem, though Timo Salonen had the system drained, and soldiered on, dragging his way up from plumb last to a sparkling fifth place at the finish.

Bruny Saby really stamped his authority on the event around the Burzet loop, which was foggy and

In 1988, as on so many previous occasions, Lancia's Monte effort was professional, clinical, and completely successful, with Frenchman Bruno Saby taking outright victory.

wet – he was 53 seconds faster than anyone else, in a 30-minute stage! – and after that his only real competition came from team-mate Yves Loubet, even though his car needed a complete transmission rebuild at one point. Alain Orielle's rally should have ended on stage eight where he put the car end-over-end, off the road, where it stayed for 20 minutes until the spectators heaved it back on to the road again!

In the meantime, J-P. Ballet's privately-prepared Peugeot 205GTI clawed its way up to third place, much to the excitement of the factory (who rushed more mechanics out to help him as the event wore on) while François Chauche eventually urged a 4WD BMW 325iX into sixth place, and to victory in the Group N category.

The only major upset, as far as Lancia was concerned, was that Yves Loubet crashed his Delta on the 14th stage, whereas Cesare Fiorio's son Alessandro had put his Delta HF 4WD securely into second place.

When the cars arrived at Monte Carlo, before taking rest and tackling the five-stage 'Mountain Circuit', the event was really already over. Saby was 10 *minutes* ahead of Fiorio, 21 *minutes* ahead of Ballet's Peugeot and 32 *minutes* ahead of Orielle's Renault 11 Turbo, which had somehow dragged its way back up to fourth place.

The rest of the rally was a formality. Though Timo Salonen's Mazda was fastest on four of the last five stages, this made no difference to the overall result, and Bruno Saby won by nearly 11 minutes.

1988

Five starting points: common route from St. Etienne

1.	B. Saby – J-F. Fauchille	(Lancia Delta HF 4WD)
2.	A. Fiorio – L. Pirollo	(Lancia Delta HF 4WD)
3.	J-P. Ballet –Ms. M-C. Lallemont	(Peugeot 205GTI)
4.	A. Orielle – J-M. Andrie	(Renault 11 Turbo)
5.	T. Salonen – S. Harjanne	(Mazda 323 4WD Turbo)
6.	F. Chauche – T. Barjou	(BMW 325iX)

169 starters, 87 finishers

Third time running for the Delta

In March 1988 Lancia homologated the Delta Integrale – a more powerful, better-braked, better handling car than the original Delta. For the rest of the year, it lost only once (in Corsica, on tarmac, where Ford's Sierra RS Cosworth was more suitable). There had never been a rallying whitewash like it.

For 1989, Lancia started as it meant to carry on, by poaching Ford's Corsica victor, Didier Auriol, and entering three Integrales for Monte Carlo rally. It was no wonder that all other teams of European cars stayed away in droves.

In 1989, however, Lancia was not guaranteed the walk-over that it had enjoyed the previous year. There were three serious challenges from Japanese cars, all of which came from teams based in Europe. Not only was Mazda Rallye Team Europe confident that its 323 Turbos were more reliable than ever before, but Toyota Team Europe was also rapidly refining the newly-developed 4WD Celica GT-Four. For the first time ever, too, Mitsubishi entered a competitive four-wheel-drive car, a Galant VR-4, driven by no less a star than Ari Vatanen.

Although 172 cars started the event, one of ten cars was likely to win: three 'works' Lancias, four 'works' or 'works-supported' Celicas, two Mazda 323s, and a singleton Mitsubishi. In any case, it was the ultra-professional 'mixture as before', with short runs from five starting points to a meeting point at St Etienne, then an eight hour rest there before tackling four stages on the way to Aubenas for a night halt. The third leg included ten special stages, and a rest halt in Digne, on the way down to Monte Carlo, where there was another night halt, and a long fourth and final leg looping out twice, from Monte Carlo, into the classic special stages in the mountains north of the Principality.

But this was still real, he-man's rallying. All in all, there were 24 special stages, totalling 613km/381 miles, with seven of those stages more than 30km/19 miles in length. If it was not quite 'office hours' rallying, this event's timing was certainly indicative of modern times. The competitors only spent two nights out of the bed (the first, before arriving at St Etienne, the second being the traditional 'last night' above Monte Carlo), and most stages were tackled in daylight.

As so often in recent years, there was very little snow on the special stages, though serious competitors still needed professional 'ice-notes' crews to chart the odd patches of ice and slush which lurked around the corners.

There was no stopping the Lancia Delta in the late eighties.

It started badly for Lancia when team manager Fiorio's son Alex (driving one of the Jolly Club Delta Integrales) lost control of his car, which ploughed into the crowd and injured two spectators. The next day it got a lot worse, when young Fiorio went off again, this time killing two spectators, one of whom was the popular Swedish driver Lars-Erik Torph.

After the first two days, Lancia's Miki Biasion and Didier Auriol were disputing the lead, with two Toyotas (Kankunnen and Carlos Sainz) close behind, and Vatanen's Mitsubishi fifth. Then, on stage nine, Toyota's challenge faded when drivers made wrong tyre choices, with Sainz going off the road and Kankunnen losing eight minutes. Waldegard's Toyota was already suffering myriad problems and (one almost wrote 'as usual') the Mazdas were off the pace.

After the restart from Digne, the newly-crowned World Champion, Biasion, rapidly began to draw away from all his rivals, and not even the local hero, Auriol, could keep in touch. It was all so predictable that the news of a team helicopter bringing down telephone wires near the Turini caused a great sensation.

On the last night, Ari Vatanen forced the big Mitsubishi into third place, then planted it off the road when he caught the accelerator pedal with his foot at the same time as he put the brakes on, while Auriol finally shrugged off puncture problems by setting fastest time on the last four stages. Even so Biasion won by 6 min. 27 sec., the fastest non-Lancia (Mikkola's Mazda) being no less than 12 min. 14 sec. off the pace.

Lancia's total domination is summed up by the 'fastest stage time' statistics – Lancia 21 (10 to Auriol, nine to Biasion, two to Saby), Toyota two (Kankunnen) and one to Mitsubishi (Vatanen)

1989

Five starting points: common route from St. Etienne.

1. M. Biasion – T. Siviero   *(Lancia Delta Integrale)*
2. D. Auriol – B. Occelli   *(Lancia Delta Integrale)*
3. B. Saby – J-F. Fauchille   *(Lancia Delta Integrale)*
4. H. Mikkola – C. Geistdorfer   *(Mazda 323 4WD Turbo)*
5. J. Kankunnen – J. Piironen   *(Toyota Celica GT-Four)*
6. P. Snyers – P. Colebunders   *(Toyota Celica GT-Four)*

172 starters, 83 finishers.